Maralene and Miles Wesner are multi-talented teachers and prolific writers. They are known for their no-nonsense style, their clear illustrations, and their willingness to face controversial issues.

From the dual perspectives of both academic and religious professions, they seek to be a bridge between the spiritual and the intellectual worlds.

Together they have published several books, articles, and studies, and both are teachers. Miles has been a bi-vocational pastor for more than 50 years. Maralene and Miles have planned and led tours and done research in all of the 50 United States, Canada, Mexico, Europe, Egypt, Japan, and the Holy Land. In 1985, they were among a small group of Americans who were invited by Dr. Joseph P. Kennedy of the US/China Education Foundation and Bishop Ting, leader of the Three Self Movement, to participate in the First Symposium on the Church in Nanjing, China.

Now, they use their lifetime of varied experiences to write insightful sermons, essays, and books.

Titles by Maralene & Miles Wesner
published by Nurturing Faith

Sermons for Special Days

Life More Abundant

Do You Really Know Jesus?

If Jesus Were Here Today

101 Sparks of Inspiration

When God Can't Answer

Think (Or Else!)

Stumbling to Zion

Sensible Sermons

Finding Truth in the Parables

The Unknown God

Truth or Tradition?

Seven Difficult Doctrines

Jesus's Commonsense Gospel

Jesus's COMMONSENSE *Gospel*

Maralene & Miles Wesner

© 2025
Published in the United States by Nurturing Faith, Macon, GA.
Nurturing Faith is a book imprint of Good Faith Media (goodfaithmedia.org).
Library of Congress Cataloging-in-Publication Data is available.

ISBN: 978-1-63528-263-4

All rights reserved. Printed in the United States of America.

Scripture quotations are from New Revised Standard Version Bible, copyright 1989, Division of Christian Education of the National Council of the Churches of Christ in the United States of America. Used by permission. All rights reserved.

Contents

Foreword 1

Tribute: A Legacy of Learning 3

About the Authors...5

Rationale 11

Introduction..15

Chapter 1: God Is Wise and Loving 31

Chapter 2: Salvation Is Free and Reasonable.....................41

Chapter 3: Doctrines Must Be Positive and Realistic 61

Chapter 4: Scripture Is Inspired, Not Inerrant.................83

Chapter 5: The Holy Spirit Makes Us Autonomous 95

Conclusion...105

Foreword

By
Bruce Gourley, Editor, *Church & State Magazine*
Former Managing Editor of Nurturing Faith Books

This book by Maralene and Miles Wesner marks a milestone. This is how they describe its purpose:

"Jesus's Commonsense Gospel is the summary and culmination of all our other work. It simply, clearly, and briefly describes the basic tenets of our faith in the way we believe Jesus would present and emphasize them if he were here today."

Long before much of modern American Christianity took a hard turn away from the inclusive Jesus of the Gospels and into an exclusive political ideology in the twenty-first century, Maralene and Miles Wesners' writings were persistently warning against the absence of Jesus in those places where the Christian faith has its strongest cultural identity.

Educators both, Maralene and Miles (he also having served as a longtime pastor as well) have been devoted to helping Christians young and old think about faith and the Bible from a standpoint of common sense, compassion, and reason.

Thinking is a friend of truth, not its enemy, they have long insisted. Miles strikes that chord again when addressing his faith journey in this book.

"Jesus realized there would be many discoveries and much more information in the future," he writes. "He knew he couldn't teach his disciples everything they would need to know."

Readers are reminded of Jesus' own words: "I still have many things to say to you, but you cannot bear them now" (John 16:12).

"It's the Holy Spirit's purpose to help believers understand and apply theological concepts in a changing world," writes Miles.

He noted Jesus saying that the Spirit will "guide you into all the truth" (John 16:13). And it is such truth that sets us free.

"That's why Christians must be able to move forward as new principles are discovered and new problems are encountered," he writes. "Change is absolutely essential if Christianity is to survive."

The Wesners have never feared new discoveries or ways of rethinking one's faith in light of fresh evidence and clearer insights into the ways Jesus called his followers to live.

In my many enjoyable conversations with Maralene over the years, she has persistently voiced passion for her and Miles's unwavering commitment to Jesus-focused Christianity. They eschew modern misrepresentations of the Christian faith that excuse or advance the exclusion and even hatred of others, instead placing Jesus-like love and inclusion at the forefront of faithful living.

At times, Maralene's voice and words convey frustration over so many professing Christians who simply ignore Jesus's teachings in the Beatitudes and his clear, prioritizing command to love God and all others as oneself.

The Wesners have long held and advocated for the fullness of religious freedom, knowing authentic faith can never be coerced.

At times, such misguided efforts have led Maralene to exclaim some variation of, "They just need to stop that and start following Jesus!"

This latest book—along with previous volumes and ongoing gifts to create the Maralene and Miles Wesners Resource Library through Belmont University—continues their life's prophetic work of calling Christianity back to Jesus.

Tribute:
A Legacy of Learning

By
John D. Pierce, Director, Jesus Worldview Initiative
Rev. Charlie Curb Center for Faith Leadership,
Belmont University

Calling professing Christians to be faithful followers of Jesus—not simply believers or admirers—is not new for Maralene and Miles Wesner. For decades their giftedness as deep thinkers and clear communicators have advanced the following of Jesus over ideologies of fear, exclusivism, and self-interest mislabeled as "Christian" or "biblical."

This concluding book echoes and expands on the all-important theme of taking seriously what Jesus said and did—and calls his followers to emulate.

Long before the Jesus Worldview Initiative emerged, less than a decade ago, the Wesners were making this central message clear to those with eyes to see and ears to hear.

"This passion isn't new for us," said Maralene. "We were already writing and publishing 'Jesus Worldview' books in the 1980s."

She noted that their book publisher at the time wasn't always supportive of their challenges to place the life and teachings of Jesus above more comfortable cultural beliefs.

"The whole Christian movement depends heavily on the person of Jesus Christ.... The distinctive features of his character are his deep humility before God, his self-dedication, his unswerving purpose and his conviction that the kingdom of God is now, and he and his followers are the agents to bring it about," wrote the Wesners in *Jesus's Message for Today: A Fresh Look at the Gospel* (1983, Broadman Press).

In a sermon Miles delivered in 1977 he stated: "Each generation has a right to reexamine and reevaluate every doctrine and practice without being branded as heretics. Christianity has nothing to fear from any genuine search for truth."

"Truth is our greatest ally, not our enemy," said Miles, noting that Jesus himself said, "I am the truth" (John 14:6).

Truth is not opinion or even cold facts, he expressed. Truthfulness is to be lived out in the following of Jesus, who revealed God to humanity through his teachings and example.

That challenge remains for followers of Jesus today, and the Wesners' good work past, present, and future provides much-needed resources for that journey. In addition to this excellent volume and previous books, Maralene and Miles are providing an ongoing opportunity to be launched this year.

The Maralene and Miles Wesner Resource Library is being developed to provide free and easy access to a wide variety of resources for teaching, preaching, and learning—focused clearly on Jesus's call to follow in his ways.

This ever-expanding online library (to be launched in 2025) is made possible by ongoing annual gifts from the Wesners to Belmont University in support of the Jesus Worldview Initiative, part of the Rev. Charlie Curb Center for Faith Leadership.

It is fitting that these longtime, honored educators and ministers would continue their legacy through a Christ-centered university and in creative ways to advance the following of Jesus as the highest Christian priority.

About the Authors

By Maralene Wesner

My spiritual journey began when I was about three or four years old, sitting on a little pink potty. All that day my family had been trying to convince my granny to let them replace her old wood-burning stove with a fancy new kerosene one. Over and over they had said, "That thing is old-timey. It's not good!" Then, suddenly, someone began to sing, "Give me that old-time religion! Give me that old-time religion! Give me that old-time religion! It's good enough for me!"

When I heard that, something clicked. I yelled, "Well, it ain't good enough for me!" If old-time stoves were bad, then why were old-time religions good? It didn't make sense! The verbal explosion and reprimands following my negative comment let me know that my opinions were not going to be respected and my crusade for logic was not going to be easy.

A few years passed, and I had become a voracious reader. I was seven or eight when I read a story about a child who went to a mission service and heard this song: "There is a fountain filled with blood, drawn from Immanuel's veins, and sinners plunged beneath that flood lose all their guilty stains."

I remember laying down my book and going out to sit on the porch swing. I thought and thought all afternoon about that strange statement. How could taking a bath in somebody's blood erase all my mistakes and fix all my problems? It didn't make sense!

My third pivotal moment came when I was about eleven. My grandfather, who had a big heart but not much religion, attended a funeral for a baby. When he came home, he'd had a few drinks and was furious. It seems the preacher had told the father that God took his baby as punishment because he wasn't attending church. Uttering a tirade of cuss words, my granddad raised his fist and shouted, "I'd never worship a god who kills babies." That very night, when my mother read her usual chapter of the Bible aloud to us, it happened to be the passage about how God "slew the first born" of every Egyptian family (see Exod 12:29). Now if he really did that, then his commandments "Thou shalt not murder" and "Love one another" are at odds with his actions. It didn't make sense!

I don't believe any religion that's based on paganistic ideas like human sacrifice and eternal torture is going to be credible in the future. I don't believe a religion that emphasizes superstitious beliefs like a donkey that scolds its master (see Num 22:28–30) and a person returning to earth from somewhere above the clouds (see Acts 1:9–11) is going to be taken seriously in the next century. It's not now!

I've read and heard every word of the Bible several times—not just the "good parts" that people quote! Some passages are shocking! Most people have no idea that this "holy, inerrant book" actually tells parents that they must have their disobedient teenagers stoned to death (see Deut 21:18–21).

The scriptures have many illogical teachings and inconsistencies, yet we're told to believe every verse, no matter how unreasonable it is. We're taught that it's sinful to question and doubt. Being conditioned to obedience and blind faith makes us vulnerable to propaganda, scam artists, and evil politicians. Individuals can't become productive citizens and democracies can't survive under these circumstances.

I believe it's past time for "new wine to be poured into new bottles." That why I want to reinterpret those Christian doctrines that are incongruous with science and technology. I feel uniquely qualified to do this because I've experienced both sides of the issue, and I've done my homework. I attended a denominational college and read every book that was available. I've taught psychology in a liberal arts university and was chosen state teacher of the year in 1975. Since I have the ability to explain things, I feel obligated and duty-bound to leave a legacy of my insights for future thinkers to build on. I want nothing in return—no money, no fame. I just need the assurance that I've done everything I can do to salvage a faith that is very important to me. Others may criticize out of hatred and a desire to destroy. I do it out of extreme concern and a desire to redeem the spiritual truth of Christianity that Jesus gave his life to preserve.

I've dealt with hundreds of puzzling questions:

(1) If the Bible was going to be the sacred guidebook for Christians, then why didn't Jesus tell his disciples about it, instead of advising them to follow their own internal guidance system known as the Holy Spirit?

(2) Why do a talking snake and a fiery hell have to be interpreted as literal and factual, but "eat my flesh" and "drink my blood" can be interpreted as symbolic?

(3) If the disciples had watched Lazarus come out of the grave after four days, why didn't they expect God to raise Jesus and wait by the tomb?

(4) Why would God set up a system of everlasting torture for multitudes of people and then tell us to love our enemies and do good to all men and women?

(5) Why does the vicarious atonement theory insist that someone has to be offered as a bloody sacrifice before God will forgive our sins?

Even as a child I desperately needed answers, so I spent the next seventy-five years of my life, my time, and my resources teaching, writing, and helping my husband pastor a small church. But my real obsession and my overriding purpose was always trying to find a religion that made sense. After decades of searching, I didn't find one, so I decided to analyze Jesus's example and teachings.

This book describes the way I believe Jesus would present the gospel if he were here today. During his time on earth, he made many improvements and updates. In fact, he went as far as he could go and did as much as he could do with the information and language that were available to him. But now Jesus expects us to go further. He said, "I still have many things to say to you, but you cannot bear them now. When the Spirit of truth comes, he will guide you into all the truth" (John 16:12–13).

We've had access to that Spirit for over two thousand years, but our religious message hasn't changed. An enormous amount of new information has been incorporated into all the other areas of life, but theology has remained the same. This commonsense gospel will present the doctrines that Jesus taught and also discover and teach some of those important "things" that he spoke about.

By Miles Wesner

Most people either deal with religion from the inside looking out or from the outside looking in.

Some individuals grow up in a traditional Christian environment with orthodox parents. They socialize with friends who have similar belief systems and moral standards. In short, they are in the position of an insider looking out and criticizing a "sinful world."

Other individuals grow up in a scientifically oriented secular environment with free-thinking parents. They associate with a diverse group of people who have varying degrees of religious and moral principles. In short, they are in a position of an outsider looking in and ridiculing a strange group of Bible-believing fanatics.

My wife and I, however, have been both in and out. I was a preacher's kid with an extremely fundamentalist lifestyle. I attended a denominational college and seminary and was pastor of a church for more than fifty years.

As a couple we didn't drink, dance, play cards, or even sew on Sunday. We tithed and were at church every time the doors were opened. Both of us carefully observed all the prescribed procedures and breathed the "sacred atmosphere" of evangelical Christianity for many years.

So we were definitely ins. Nevertheless, we are also definitely outs. Both of us constantly questioned orthodox theology. We earned graduate degrees from Oklahoma University with classes in philosophy and psychology. We wrote academic programs and served as educational consultants. We traveled the fifty states and over thirty foreign countries, meeting Muslims, visiting with rabbis, and interacting with agnostics and atheists. The fact that we have experienced life from both very different viewpoints gives us a unique ability to evaluate the validity of religion from the inside looking out and from the outside looking in.

We are spending our final years recording our impressions and attempting to correlate the insights we have gained from these two diametrically opposed perspectives.

Because of our intensive study of the Gospels and our own real-life experiences, we've realized that Christianity, as it's being taught, does not reflect Jesus's values. We've also learned that only a small percentage of non-Christians have a good impression of Christianity.

Our world is changing. In the past a minister could use shame, guilt, and fear to motivate members. On Sundays pastors could expect the faithful to sit through a forty-five-minute sermon, whether it related to their life or not. Now, when people come to church, they want honesty and reality. Their marriages, their families, and their jobs are stressful. They're willing to get involved in church only if doing so will help them solve their personal problems.

To deal with this situation, we've always offered practical principles and utilized different methods. We don't use a lot of pious, religious language. We don't emphasize miraculous events. We don't waste our time denouncing specific sins.

We're very tolerant of different beliefs and lifestyles. We're open to any seeking person. We encourage ordinary men and women to be God's agents here on earth. We present the type of whole-life gospel that Jesus taught. This includes basic life skills, good relationships, and the productive use of talents and resources.

Since we only have a few years of active life left, we want to make the most of them. There are many churches that teach traditional doctrines, but there are very few churches that serve non-traditionalists, so we are reaching out to those searchers and thinkers who are often ostracized. We believe many productive, honest people reject Christianity because they can't accept the doctrines as they are being taught. That's why we advocate Jesus's "commonsense gospel."

Rationale

When Jesus made drastic changes in religious beliefs and moral standards, the orthodox priests and pious leaders accused him of destroying their faith. He changed the idea of God from physical to spiritual (see John 4:24). He rejected many Sabbath-day regulations. He relaxed rules about fasting and handwashing. He ridiculed long prayers and other worship practices. In fact, he never presented a formal creed or advocated an organized doctrinal system. Instead, he emphasized the acceptance of sinners and counseled individuals! His advice to Nicodemus about conversion was totally different from his advice to the rich young ruler.

Even Paul, who tended to be more concerned about proper morality codes than Jesus was, admitted that he often adjusted his own behavior to deal with the different beliefs and customs of his associates. When he was with people who understood that idols are not real, then he ate the meat that had been offered to them. But when he was with superstitious people who thought eating such meat was wrong, then he refrained from eating it (see 1 Cor 8:4–18).

Paul also described how he adapted his teachings to various cultural groups, saying,

> To the Jews I became as a Jew, in order to gain Jews. To those under the law I became as one under the law (though I myself am not under the law) so that I might gain those under the law. To those outside the law I became as one outside the law (though I am not outside God's law but am within Christ's law) so that I might gain those outside the law. To the weak I became weak,

> so that I might gain the weak. I have become all things to all people, that I might by all means save some. (1 Cor 9:20–22)

Paul realized he had to make major changes in his evangelistic approach to reach different groups of people.

If both Jesus and Paul could adapt the gospel to meet the current needs of their constituents, then why can't we do that?

For two thousand years, and especially since the canonization of our current Bible, Christians have been forced to express the gospel message with the same basic explanatory phrases and from the same predetermined format. Anyone who dares to reinterpret or update doctrines is labeled a heretic. Christian theology remains stuck in the past while everything else in the world moves on. We're prevented from developing new insights or utilizing new information. We're required to repeat the same time-worn precepts.

As a result, we're losing generations of people. Our presentation of the gospel is completely outdated, irrelevant, and unreasonable to many individuals in the twenty-first century. Americans and citizens of most other countries have not been reared in an environment of masters and slaves or monarchs and subjects. They have not been taught from birth that we must appease a supernatural deity by killing and burning animals as sacrifices. Phrases such as the *vicarious atonement* are like foreign languages to most people living in a scientific age. If we say Jesus paid for your sins, a sensible person might ask, "Who did he pay? Was it God? Was it Satan? Was it some unknown 'keeper of the books'?"

Did anyone pay for the prodigal son's sins? Payment isn't mentioned in Jesus's parable. That father simply loved and accepted him with no demands whatsoever.

Also, Jesus told us to forgive freely and constantly (see Matt 18:22). So why did someone have to die for God to forgive our sins?

In ancient times these issues of payment for sin and propitiation were relevant and meaningful. Threats of God's wrath and warnings of punishment caused guilt and fear among the people. These negative feelings and beliefs needed to be eliminated. That's why explaining Jesus's life and death in that context was liberating. It gave Paul such relief and assurance that extreme grace became his theme. But this complicated rationale of depravity and atonement is not a part of people's lives today and has not been for centuries. We must be allowed to reinterpret the gospel in a way that ordinary men and women can understand. We must be allowed to express the plan of salvation in words that meet current needs. That's why Jesus said, "New wine must be put into new wineskins."

It's significant that both Jesus and Paul realized the necessity for change. This should give us permission to adapt doctrines and teachings for a modern audience. Jesus realized there would be many discoveries and much more information in the future. He knew he couldn't teach his disciples everything they would need to know. It's the Holy Spirit's purpose to help believers understand and apply theological concepts in a changing world. He also said it's the truth that will make us free. That's why Christians must be able to move forward as new principles are discovered and new problems are encountered. Change is essential if Christianity is to survive.

Jesus was interested in theological and moral issues throughout his life. At age twelve he was already discussing these things with adults in the temple. The scriptures say, "After three days they found him in the temple, sitting among the teachers, listening to them and asking them questions. And all who heard him were amazed at his understanding and his answers" (Luke 2:46–47). Putting new wine in new bottles requires drastic changes. In Palestine two thousand years ago, Jesus went about as far as he could go with the information that was available to him. But if he were here today, he would go further. He also used the language of his time and place because that's all he had, but if he were here today, he would use the language that is understood in this time and place. For instance, medical terms would replace "demon possessions," and scientific terms would replace superstitious explanations. But nothing can ever replace his basic teachings about truth, love, forgiveness, and concern for others.

During his years of ministry, Jesus always offered a commonsense religious system. After evaluating all the possible rituals and creeds, he settled for a simple, logical format with no complicated theology, no useless requirements, and no complex mysteries. He just said, "You shall love the Lord your God with all your heart and with all your soul and with all your mind. This is the greatest and first commandment. And a second is like it: You shall love your neighbor as yourself. On these two commandments hang all the Law and the Prophets" (Matt 22:36–40).

We believe if Jesus were here today, his message and mission would be based on these two verses. Therefore, this book presents a framework for such a commonsense gospel.

Introduction

Before we decide what Jesus would teach about doctrines, we must get to know his personality and understand his mission and purpose.

Christians have allowed art and literature to create a distorted image of Jesus. He was not a meek cardboard figure floating around in white robes and a halo. He was a tough activist, strong enough to physically remove the hypocritical religious leaders who cheated the poor people worshiping in the temple. He was a real person with passionate feelings of love, joy, and hope but also of frustration, impatience, anger, sorrow, and despair. A more human profile of such a unique man will enable us to identify with him and follow his example as we make decisions about our own personal morality and social relationships.

Above all else, Jesus was compassionate and generous. He loved God and served others. He offered assurances of grace repeatedly as he interacted with both individuals and groups. In his ministry to hurting people, he avoided and in fact ridiculed empty pious language, saying, "Not everyone who says to me, 'Lord, Lord,' will enter the kingdom of heaven, but only the one who does the will of my Father in heaven" (Matt 7:21–22).

Jesus was careful about what he did say. He clearly expressed the idea that words matter, saying, "Let your word be 'Yes, yes' or 'No, no'; anything more than this comes from the evil one" (Matt 5:37).

He also said, "On the day of judgment you will have to give an account for every careless word you utter" (Matt 12:36).

Strangely enough, sometimes it's what people *don't* say that's more significant than what they *do* say. That may be true of Jesus. When Jesus met Nicodemus (see John 3), we might have expected him to say,

"Rabbi, I really appreciate your interest in my message. I'm honored that a man with your theological knowledge, ethical ideals, and high position would want to visit with me."

Yes, he might have said something like this, but he didn't. He opened the discussion with some blunt advice. He told Nicodemus that he couldn't depend on his physical birth lineage from Abraham. He explained that unless a person gets a different outlook on life and has a new birth of spiritual understanding they can't enter or even recognize the kingdom of God (see John 3:3–16).

When Jesus met the rich young ruler (see Matt 19:16–22), we might have expected him to say, "You are a remarkably moral and responsible individual. You deserve great respect for being so obedient and faithful. Few people keep all the commandments as you have done. However, if you really want to serve God, you should sell your possessions and come follow me. We could certainly use your money in my ministry."

Yes, he might have said this. Today, most evangelists and religious leaders would welcome such a wealthy seeker. But Jesus didn't! He asked for nothing and advised him to donate his riches to the poor. Furthermore, he didn't pressure him to join his group of disciples or criticize him because he chose to walk away.

When Jesus met the woman at the well (see John 4:7–29), we might have expected him to say, "Lady, you're immoral. I've never seen such a messed-up life. You've had five husbands, and now you're living with some guy and don't even claim to be married. If you repent, leave your sinful relationships, and show proper conduct, then perhaps I'll try to help you."

Yes, you'd think he would have at least mentioned her sinful lifestyle, but he didn't. He simply offered her living water.

When Jesus met the Roman centurion (see Matt 8:5–10), we might have expected him to say, "Hey, Mister, surely you don't expect me to heal your servant or do anything else for you. It's against our Jewish law for me to even enter your house. God doesn't hear or answer the prayers of pagans. You must repudiate your allegiance to Caesar. You must study our Torah, accept our doctrines, and obey our commandments before you can receive any help from me."

Yes, he might have said all this and more, but he didn't. He graciously offered to visit his home, praised his faith, and healed his servant.

When Jesus met Zacchaeus (see Luke 19:1–10), he might have said, "You traitor! You have lied and cheated people for years. You must change your profession and find some way to make an honest living before I can even associate with you."

Yes, he might have responded like this, but he didn't. Instead, he immediately offered him fellowship and friendship.

When Jesus met the Canaanite woman who asked him to heal her daughter (see Matt 15:22–28), we might have expected him to say, "You're a Gentile. You don't have the correct background or religious beliefs or moral standards. I can't help you. Besides all that, you're a foreigner. You don't deserve God's blessings."

Yes, he might have reacted in that negative and critical manner, but he didn't. As if to test her, he said, "It's not fair to give the children's food to the dogs." Then, when she dared to respond with a clever and rather impudent retort, saying, "Yes, but even dogs are allowed to eat the crumbs," instead of a reprimand, he complimented and rewarded her.

When Jesus met the many prostitutes, criminals. and other sinners, we might have expected him to immediately present the salvation formula to each one of them. But he didn't! If people who do not repent and believe in the death, burial, and resurrection of Jesus are going to be punished forever, then why did he fail to explain this clearly at every opportunity?

Why didn't he say, "You must reject your unorthodox religious notions. You must believe that I'm going to die to pay for your sins. You must accept me into your heart." It seems unbelievable that Jesus would omit these critical life-giving words if they are necessary to save individuals from eternal damnation. Surely he wouldn't be negligent about such a crucial matter, yet Jesus failed to give this essential gospel message. He didn't urge people to make the personal decision for Christ that evangelicals demand today. He never asked would-be converts to pray the sinner's prayer or to repeat it after him.

Most Christian groups base their doctrines on the "repent, believe, accept" model of salvation. They consider it to be an absolute requirement. But Jesus didn't mention it to anyone. He didn't say it to Nicodemus. He didn't say it to the rich young ruler. He didn't say it to the woman at the well, the Roman centurion, Zacchaeus, or the Canaanite woman. Instead of criticism, requirements, and warnings, in each case Jesus just offered immediate acceptance, forgiveness, and hope. That's the gospel! That's why what he didn't say is so significant!

It's obvious that a Christian gospel should be based on the beliefs, values, teachings, and practices of Jesus the Christ, but that's not always true in churches today.

Jesus was practical. He ridiculed many of the elaborate rules and rituals that were prevalent at that time. He said, "Words are useless unless you walk your talk." He explained that the Sabbath was made for our benefit, so if you are hungry on the Sabbath, pick grain to eat; if an ox falls into a ditch on the Sabbath, pull him out.

He said giving cups of cold water (see Mark 9:41) and reconciling social conflicts (see Matt 5:23–24) may be more important elements of worship than saying prayers and singing hymns.

Contrary to popular stereotypes Jesus was not a religious fanatic. He led a normal, balanced life and was criticized for it.

He certainly presented a radically different gospel. When he called Matthew, a hated tax collector, to be his disciple and then chose to eat with a group of especially wicked sinners, the pious Pharisees were critical. When they attacked him, Jesus gave a startling reply, saying, "Those who are well have no need of a physician, but those who are sick" (Matt 9:12).

Another group, who were followers of John the Baptist, questioned his liberal tendencies, saying, "Why do we and the Pharisees fast often, but your disciples do not fast?" (Matt 9:14).

Jesus responded with two profound analogies, which indicated that he was developing and promoting an entirely different belief system. He said, "No one sews a piece of unshrunk cloth on an old cloak, for the patch pulls away from the cloak, and a worse tear is made. Neither is new wine put into old wineskins; otherwise, the skins burst, and the wine is spilled, and the skins are ruined, but new wine is put into fresh wineskins, and so both are preserved" (Matt 9:16–17).

Jesus was explaining that you can't continue putting new patches on old threadbare garments. You can't keep pouring new wine into old, brittle wineskins. There comes a time when total renovation is required.

For two thousand years theologians have been trying to sew patches of new discoveries and insights on the ragged fabric of outdated orthodoxy. This is a waste of time and resources.

For two thousand years religious leaders have been trying to pour the new wine of fresh thoughts and ideas into the worn-out wineskins of outdated traditional creeds. This too is a waste of time and resources.

Early Christians made drastic changes as they adapted to non-Hebrew groups, with their different beliefs and customs. Their requirements for circumcision and food taboos were modified as they integrated with Gentiles, but modern Christians haven't been allowed to do that. We've been forced to stand and mark time at the canon barrier. Many elements of the gospel being preached today are irrelevant and illogical. Our theology can't be touched up or given a facelift. Much of it is passe and useless. Jesus knew false teachings and obsolete notions must be replaced. He realized that when later generations had to deal with unexpected situations and solve new problems, changes would be necessary. In his description of old cloth and old wineskins, he was giving us permission to make these changes.

Even so, tampering with religion can be frightening and controversial. Almost everyone, even individuals who have never professed any faith or engaged in any worship practices, will often cling desperately to the tenets of their forefathers and resist change.

Nevertheless, some of us must be willing to express disturbing viewpoints. Some of us must present transformational ideas. Some of us must have the courage to face opposition and act, because at this moment in time new wine is essential if Christianity is to remain credible and influential.

What if we were forced to still cook exactly like Martha and Mary cooked? What if we were told we must travel just like Paul and Barnabas traveled? What if we had to communicate by writing on scrolls like Matthew and Mark did?

It's strange that theology is the only area of life that has been required to cease all growth and remain the same as it was two thousand years ago.

Scientists are not restricted to the information that was available to them in 30 A.D. Medical experts aren't still relying on ancient herbal remedies. No one hinders the growth of knowledge in space exploration or cancer research or military strategies. Inventors are not punished for making improvements in their mechanical devices. Innovators are not burned at the stake if additional facts force them to make adjustments in their current methods. Changes in technology are not only accepted; they're encouraged. But in religion nothing must ever change! Yet Jesus dared to advocate for new wine in new bottles.

Surprisingly, when we analyze Jesus's new wine, we find that it doesn't lead us to more complicated theological creeds or more elaborate worship ceremonies. A careful examination of Jesus's words and deeds reveals a simple, commonsense gospel.

To introduce this new cloth and this new wine, we must study Jesus's teachings and lifestyle. This will help us follow his example. Remember, John said, "As he is, so are we in this world" (1 John 4:17).

Jesus's life in Palestine in the first century was drastically different from our life in America today, yet we're told we must emulate his beliefs and actions. That can be difficult to do because we must rely on the sketchy biographical information presented in the four Gospels. Trying to discover and salvage clues concerning Jesus's true character and message is a real challenge. Nevertheless, it's possible to consider the few isolated incidents that were recorded and then extrapolate the truth from them. We can say, "Since he reacted that way then, if he were here today, he would probably react this way now." Such comparisons require deep thought and a lot of time and effort, but if we're honest and persistent, we'll be able to get enough insights to change the world!

Many sincere Christians fail to follow Jesus's advice, even on minor matters. For instance, so often today, congregations believe that church worship should involve chanting praise choruses repeatedly and ending with raised hands and shouts of "hallelujah!" Yet we have evidence that Jesus ridiculed and rejected such performances. He didn't appreciate long prayers, saying, "When you are praying, do not heap up empty phrases as the gentiles do, for they think that they will be heard because of their many words" (Matt 6:7).

One interesting incident illustrates his opinion about sanctimonious jargon and emotional worship expressions. The scriptures say, "A woman in the crowd raised her voice and said to him, 'Blessed is the womb that bore you and the breasts that nursed you!'" Now this woman was probably sincere, but instead of being pleased with her adoration, Jesus replied, "Blessed rather are those who hear the word of God and obey it!" (Luke 11:27–28).

Jesus preferred plain rather than pompous speech. Almost all his messages and lessons consisted of interesting stories and thoughtful discussions. He didn't orate. He just talked, and he usually did this from an informal seated position. The scriptures often say, "All the people came to him, and he sat down and began to teach them" (John 8:2).

If we're supposed to follow Jesus's behavior, then why do so many modern evangelistic meetings consist of loud sermonic rants accompanied by pulpit pounding and Bible waving? That's more "human drama" than "biblical precept."

It's hard to really know a person who lived so long ago, but the Gospels do provide enough often overlooked vignettes to give us valuable information about Jesus's character, values, and methods of ministry. These can help us determine what he would say and do now about current issues.

One significant episode occurred when Jesus was only twelve years old. The family traveled to Jerusalem, and he got separated from his parents. When his mother scolded him, he said, "Did you not know that I must be in my Father's house?" (Luke 2:49).

This encounter shows us that Jesus was always interested in serious matters and enjoyed an exchange of ideas. He would still encourage intelligent, inquisitive young people to ask questions and express their opinions.

Jesus was a precocious child, but he also identified with common people. Many religious groups require their members to wear special clothing, avoid certain foods, and adhere to specific rules and regulations, but Jesus didn't do that!

In his comparison to John the Baptist, he emphasized that Christians are not expected to have strange lifestyles or to perform odd rituals. He said, "For John came neither eating nor drinking, and they say, 'He has a demon'; the Son of Man came eating and drinking, and they say, 'Look, a glutton and a drunkard, a friend of tax collectors and sinners!'" (Matt 11:18–19).

Jesus's response to these petty criticisms proves that his lifestyle was normal. There is no evidence that he was ever considered to be especially religious. He attended public events, celebrated weddings, and socialized with worldly people (see John 2:1–11).

He advocated family gatherings with food, music, dancing, and fellowship (see Luke 15:23–25).

He worked hard but also made time for recreation, meditation, and relaxation (see Luke 5:16; 6:12). It's interesting to note that Jesus was such an ordinary looking and acting individual that officials had to pay Judas to point him out in the crowd (see Matt 26:47–50).

But Jesus also welcomed diversity. His concern for others included all races and religions. He said, "People will come from east and west, from north and south, and take their places at the banquet in the kingdom of God" (Luke 13:29). That statement is important because in this culture eating together indicated social compatibility and equality.

Jesus had no patience with segregation. He never honored a caste system. On the contrary, he always championed the underdog and honored the least of these. Most of his parables made heroes of sinners, lepers, Samaritans, Romans, and foreigners. He also greatly elevated the status of women and children.

We know that Jesus loved everybody, but he also had special affection for certain individuals. The rich young ruler refused his invitation and walked away, but the scripture says, "Jesus, looking at him, loved him" (Mark 10:21).

The scripture also says, "Jesus loved Martha and her sister and Lazarus." They were his close friends, and he enjoyed their fellowship (see John 11:5).

When Jesus was on the cross, the scripture says, "When Jesus saw his mother and the disciple whom he loved standing beside her, he said to his mother, 'Woman, here is your son'" (John 19:26).

Jesus was a people person. He even had empathy for large groups of stubborn people who refused his help. He said, "Jerusalem, Jerusalem, the city that kills the prophets and stones those who are sent to it! How often have I desired to gather your children together as a hen gathers her brood under her wings, and you were not willing!" (Matt 23:37).

Jesus was a passionate individual, and he always expressed his honest emotions. He was often impatient, and he could be angry! Sometimes he was sorrowful, and he certainly gave Christians permission to grieve. At Lazarus's tomb "Jesus began to weep" (John 11:35).

When tragedies occurred, Jesus never quoted shallow platitudes. Today, he wouldn't tell a broken-hearted mother, "God needed your baby in heaven."

He revealed his depression and negative feelings in the garden of Gethsemane. The scripture says, "[He] began to be grieved and agitated" (Matt 26:37).

Jesus also gave us the right to question God. Like the psalmist, Jeremiah, and a few other prophets, he dared to voice doubts and complaints. He prayed one especially desperate prayer, saying, "My God, my God, why have you forsaken me?" (Matt 27:46).

Jesus was persecuted and rejected. Herod wanted to kill him while he was still an infant (see Matt 2:13). His neighbors tried to throw him off a cliff when he preached his first sermon (see Luke 4:29).

The Pharisees and Sadducees hated him. Crowds ridiculed him. Judas betrayed him. Peter denied him. His disciples abandoned him. Soldiers crucified him.

Jesus didn't let these difficulties defeat him, but he didn't continue to waste his time and effort on useless projects either. Once, he gave some practical advice, saying, "Do not give what is holy to dogs, and do not throw your pearls before swine, or they will trample them under foot and turn and maul you" (Matt 7:6).

He was also willing to cut his losses, adapt to circumstances, and change course when necessary, saying, "If anyone will not welcome you or listen to your words, shake off the dust from your feet as you leave that house or town" (Matt 10:14). In other words, he is advising us to leave our past behind. He doesn't want us to berate ourselves for mistakes and failures or to be overcome by obsessive guilt and regret.

Jesus was not especially idealistic, but he was sensitive and sympathetic. He told numerous parables about the selfish use of money and possessions. His hardest hitting illustration described a miser who neglected a poor beggar. He said, "There was a rich man who was dressed in purple and fine linen and who feasted sumptuously every day. And at his gate lay a poor man named Lazarus, covered with sores" (Luke 16:19–20).

After the rich man and the beggar died, Jesus quoted Abraham as saying to the rich man, "during your lifetime you received your good things and Lazarus in like manner evil things, but now he is comforted here, and you are in agony" (Luke 16:25).

He even shocked people by saying, "It will be hard for a rich person to enter the kingdom of heaven" (Matt 19:23). If he were here today, he wouldn't con people out of their money or condone the behavior of some televangelists and megachurch pastors who ride around in limousines, live in mansions, and preach a prosperity gospel.

In an incident involving a tax ruling, Jesus was willing to compromise. The scripture says, "Once a tax collector asked Peter, 'Doesn't your teacher pay the temple tax?' He answered, 'Yes.' Later, Jesus spoke to him about it, saying, 'Simon, do rulers collect taxes from their own children, or from others?' Peter said, 'From other people.' Jesus said, 'Then the sons are exempt. However, in order to avoid trouble, we will pay the tax'" (Matt 17:24–27).

In this case, even though Jesus felt the law was unjust, he chose to comply rather than create an unnecessary conflict.

We learn from this and many other such examples that not every question in life has an absolutely right or absolutely wrong answer. Situational ethics is still a debated topic among many Christians, but Jesus's general response was always to place people over rules and love above law.

Jesus was logical and reasonable. For instance, when John the Baptist had doubts and sent men to question him about his identity and position of authority, he didn't quote scriptural prophecy or give an emotional defense. He simply said, "Go and tell John what you hear and see" (Matt 11:4). In other words, "trust your eyes and ears" and "examine the evidence."

If a traditional doctrine or practice leads to confusion or harmful consequences, then it should be discarded. Studying these and other seemingly insignificant incidents gives us glimpses into Jesus's general attitude, thinking patterns, and techniques of operation. It enables us to develop and present a commonsense gospel that can be understood and applied in our modern world.

For thousands of years fanatical religious leaders have been trying to make people accept complicated and irrational systems of belief. Each group has different requirements and rituals. Each group claims their demands come straight from the mouth of their god. Each group uses threats and rewards to ensure obedience.

Things are changing today. As scientists learn about the natural processes of our world and as people mature and have greater access to knowledge, it's becoming more and more difficult for religious gurus to attract followers and maintain their allegiance. The overall influence of religion is diminishing.

Jesus knew this could happen. That's probably why he described two possible paths to faith. He said, "Believe me that I am in the Father and the Father is in me, but if you do not, then believe because of the works themselves" (John 14:11).

Jesus was astute. He realized that people are different. Some individuals are content to follow traditional teachings. They are comfortable with the status quo. They don't ask questions or express doubts. Such men and women can often live moral, productive lives. They may be satisfied simply to believe.

Others, however, cannot do this. They are more analytical and logical. They need evidence and reasons for their beliefs. Jesus respected this outlook. That's why he advised them to evaluate his ministry of service to believe.

The search for truth is different for everyone. People are like potted plants. Each of us has a faith container. The size of that container isn't important for those men and women whose roots never touch the sides of the vessel. The size of the faith container is crucial, however, for those individuals with a lot of potential for growth. For instance, planting an herb in a cup is okay, but planting an acorn in a cup is asking for trouble!

When a person's belief system isn't large enough or flexible enough to allow for continual growth, one of two things will happen: If the container is weak and shoddy, it will crack under the strain. When such a shattered faith container has to be discarded, the resulting disillusionment often leads to atheism and cynicism.

If, on the other hand, the faith container is strong and rigid, it will limit the growth and force the intellectual roots into grotesque distortions! Small, inflexible faith containers stifle productivity and cause perversion. Many of our worst addicts and criminals come from this group of frustrated individuals. That's why each of us must have a faith container that allows us to grow and reach our full potential.

Most religions and churches seem to favor small, rigid faith containers that don't encourage or even accept deep thinkers. This commonsense gospel is for those alienated individuals.

Even the scriptures themselves can produce moral dissonance. If we take certain passages seriously, we'll be forced to examine and question many traditional assumptions.

One such scripture records Jesus's own words: "God is spirit, and those who worship him must worship in spirit and truth" (John 4:24).

If God is spiritual or abstract rather than anthropomorphic or concrete, then maybe we should rethink our theology.

To understand this verse we need to know what *spirit* means. In the original Hebrew and Greek, it meant "like breath or like air." What characteristics does this suggest? Air is everywhere, and yet it's nowhere! It can't be located geographically. It takes many shapes and forms. It can't be delineated or pictured. You can't see it or touch it or capture it. It's an invisible force that's unseen but real. It's there, but under normal conditions you're unaware of it. You take advantage of it constantly, but you don't appreciate it until you lose it.

Another thought-provoking scripture also records Jesus's own words: "The kingdom of God is not coming with things that can be observed, nor will they say, 'Look, here it is!' or 'There it is!' For, in fact, the kingdom of God is among you" (Luke 17:20–21).

If the kingdom is a psychological concept rather than a physical location out there in the ether, then maybe we should rethink our doctrines.

To understand this verse we need to know what *among* means. In the original Hebrew and Greek, it meant "in the midst of or in your soul or within you."

If so, then the kingdom of God is something that is personalized rather than standardized. Each person will realize it differently. It's significant that Jesus didn't say, "The sun is among [or within] you" or "The mountain is among [or within] you." These are tangible, concrete objects. All people see them and react to them. They exist independently of human beings, but Jesus did say, "The kingdom is among [or within] you." It's not a place. It's not an entity. It isn't the same to everyone. If the kingdom is among us or within us, then we know that the kingdom doesn't involve Israel or Jerusalem. It doesn't foretell a coming in the clouds. It's not something that's being set up in a heavenly sphere.

When Jesus prayed "May your kingdom come. May your will be done on earth as it is in heaven" (Matt 6:10), he was expressing his desire for God's will and therefore God's kingdom to become a reality in the lives of believers in this world.

Another disturbing scripture records Paul's admonition concerning right and wrong. He says, "I know and am persuaded in the Lord Jesus that nothing is unclean in itself, but it is unclean for anyone who considers it unclean" (Rom 14:14).

If morality is conditionally determined, rather than being based on principles that are external and absolute, then maybe we should rethink the entire theme of Christianity.

These are questions that require open minds and profound thoughts. But is anybody willing to discuss them or deal with them? Once, in a meeting concerning the ordination of women, the archbishop of Canterbury said, "I agree in principle, but I feel such a move right now would divide the church."

Does that viewpoint reflect prudence or cowardice? It depends! Jesus said, "Do you think that I have come to bring peace to the earth? No, I tell you, but rather division! From now on five in one household will be divided, three against two and two against three" (Luke 12:51–52). Jesus certainly wasn't advocating conflict. Far from it, he was deeply committed to harmony and unity, but he was not committed to "peace at any price." He knew there will always come a time when truth and justice must take precedence over harmony and unity. Abraham Lincoln didn't want to instigate a horrible civil war, but he knew there comes a time when action is necessary.

No one likes a troublemaker who constantly stirs up strife and dissension, or an ideologue who uses his convictions to condemn everyone who differs, or a prankster who rocks the boat just for the fun of it. Nevertheless, if the captain is asleep, if the sailors are neglecting their duties, and if the vessel is on a collision course with an immovable object, then to save that craft full of passengers, sometimes rocking the boat may be necessary! The problem is to know when to rock it! We should never cause division over petty personal slights. Jesus said to forgive and turn the other cheek on those occasions (see Matt 5:39).

We should never cause division over minor problems of terminology or labels. When the disciples met a group who did good works but were not identified as his followers, Jesus said, "Do not stop him, for no one who does a deed of power in my name will be able soon afterward to speak evil of me. Whoever is not against us is for us" (Mark 9:39–40).

If we're never to rock the boat or cause division over trivial issues, then when should we rock the boat? Good people have often let things slide and compromised their integrity because they "hated to cause trouble." Does this attitude reflect prudence or cowardice? It's a matter of priorities. It's determined by deciding what's important and what's not, and there are no easy answers.

Jesus was accepting, tolerant, and loving, but he could also be condemning, intolerant, and harsh. He ignored many slights, attacks, and threats. Once, when a Samaritan village would not receive them, Jesus's disciples said, "Lord, do you want us to command fire to come down from heaven and consume them?" Jesus scolded them, and they went on to another village (see Luke 9:51–56).

We see that Jesus overlooked most insults and compromised on certain customs and regulations, but he never hesitated to rock the boat when human values were at stake. The scriptures say, "On another Sabbath he entered the synagogue and taught, and there was a man there whose right hand was withered. The scribes and the Pharisees were watching him to see whether he would cure on the Sabbath…. He said to him, 'Stretch out your hand.' He did so, and his hand was restored.

But they were filled with fury and began discussing with one another what they might do to Jesus" (Luke 6:6–7, 10–11).

When someone asked, "Why do your disciples break the tradition of the elders? For they do not wash their hands before they eat," Jesus explained, "'It is not what goes into the mouth that defiles a person, but it is what comes out of the mouth that defiles.' Then the disciples approached and said to him, 'Do you know that the Pharisees took offense when they heard what you said?'" (Matt 15:2, 11–12). In this case Jesus wasn't deliberately trying to offend the Pharisees, but he was remaining true to his values.

Jesus detested hypocrisy, saying, "Woe to you, scribes and Pharisees, hypocrites! For you are like whitewashed tombs, which on the outside look beautiful but inside are full of the bones of the dead and of all kinds of uncleanness" (Matt 23:27).

He detested double standards, saying, "Woe also to you experts in the law! For you load people with burdens hard to bear, and you yourselves do not lift a finger to ease them" (Luke 11:46).

He detested oppression, saying, "Woe to you, scribes and Pharisees, hypocrites! For you lock people out of the kingdom of heaven. For you do not go in yourselves, and when others are going in you stop them" (Matt 23:13).

Jesus's only recorded act of physical violence was the one directed toward those self-righteous leaders who cheated people and used religion for material gain. When Jesus entered the temple and found merchants selling oxen and sheep and doves and the moneychangers seated at their table, he made a whip of cords and drove them all out of the temple, saying, "My house shall be called a house of prayer, but you are making it a den of robbers" (Matt 21:13; see also John 2:13–18).

Jesus realized that sometimes the boat needs rocking!

Teaching that God is wise and loving will probably rock the boat.

Teaching that salvation is free and reasonable will probably rock the boat.

Teaching that doctrines must be positive and realistic will probably rock the boat.

Teaching that scriptures are inspired but not inerrant will probably rock the boat.

Teaching that the Holy Spirit within makes us autonomous will probably rock the boat.

Nevertheless, all these important beliefs must be included in Jesus's commonsense gospel!

Chapter 1:

God Is Wise and Loving

The gospel being preached today has innumerable problems and inconsistencies. Even though most people don't realize it, the atonement theory itself presents a negative description of God. It seems to depict him as a blood-thirsty despot who requires the death of something or someone before he will forgive sin. It also warns us that he has prepared a fiery, everlasting torture chamber for every human being who doesn't believe in this theory. This deity also appears to be extremely jealous and narcissistic, requiring submissive attitudes and constant adoration from his subjects.

Since ordinary men and women are more ethical and humane than such a deity, this view of God creates doubts, confusion, and uncertainty.

Jesus totally rejects any beliefs and doctrines that portray a negative profile of the God he calls "Abba, Father" (Mark 14:36).

So if our gospel is flawed and difficult to understand, what is the solution?

Some people ignore it, forget it, or reject it, but let's not throw out the baby with the bath water. Human beings do need spiritual connections. Human beings do need moral guidelines. Human beings do need assurance and hope. None of the current established religions are filling these basic needs, but there is a simple solution. Maybe we should stop and consider what a wise and loving creator would really want his people to do. Maybe we should stop and consider what a wise and loving father would really want his children to do.

Would a compassionate deity compile a list of trivial rules and regulations and then impose harsh penalties for those who break them? Would an intelligent deity require individuals to participate in elaborate ceremonies and rituals that have no practical purpose? Would a benevolent deity command everyone to constantly bow before him with effusive praise and obeisance?

I don't think so!

Many teachings in traditional Christianity are not reasonable. They originated from ancient traditions and are based upon autocratic conditions. Most Christians believe God is love (see 1 John 4:16). Most Christians believe God is righteous (see Neh 9:8). But sometimes we forget God is also smart! We often attribute words and actions to God that are not sensible, logical, or intelligent. If he is trying to convey "the wisdom of the universe" to human beings through an inerrant scripture, why would he include so much trivial material about the exact measurements of the ark of the covenant? Why would he describe the minute details of the priests' garments? Why would he introduce strange terms like *anti-Christ*s and *marks of the beast* when he knew this would cause distractions and be misinterpreted?

A God who is intelligent enough to create atoms and gravity would not concoct a system that required someone to be killed as a sacrifice before sins could be forgiven. He would not set up an everlasting torture chamber for all those who don't agree with this system.

An intelligent God would not command that a specific Sabbath day must be observed, because he would know that days are not the same all around the earth. For instance, it's not the Sabbath in Japan when it's the Sabbath in England. And a day on the space capsule is entirely different.

An intelligent God would know that supernatural miracles can only occur when divine laws contradict natural laws, and that sets up a dangerous precedent. The worst thing that can happen to a gambling addict is to win occasionally. If results are not linked to causes, this tempts people to take more risks, hoping for that rare exception.

We're told to glorify God, and that means to make God look good. We certainly aren't doing that when we proclaim things about God that make him appear to be erratic, inconsistent, and unintelligent.

The doctrine of depravity and original sin is illogical. It's obvious that most human beings are not evil and depraved. The species would not have survived if that were the case. Sure, we are born with selfish tendencies, and since we learn through trial and error, we do make a lot of mistakes. But most individuals also have a basic sense of fairness and feel empathy and concern for each other. In tragic situations, even criminals will often sacrifice for children. As someone said, "There's a touch of honor even among thieves."

That's why trying to convince people that every person on this earth is evil enough and sinful enough to deserve eternal punishment just because a primitive couple made one poor choice is not logical. It doesn't make sense!

Babies are not born depraved. Jesus said that we should become like little children (see Matt 18:3–4). Ezekiel also repudiated the idea of inherited sin, saying, "The person who sins shall die. A child shall not suffer for the iniquity of a parent" (Ezek 18:20).

A loving creator would never set up a system of everlasting torture that has no redeeming features. Such vengeance doesn't rehabilitate or eliminate evil. It perpetuates and increases evil. That's not logical. It doesn't make sense!

A fair-minded creator would never impose cruel punishment on people for not accepting his son as their savior, especially if they had never even heard of him. Such a "worse than death sentence," which keeps people alive in misery forever, would have doomed billions of men and women from early times until now. That's not logical. It doesn't make sense!

A moral creator would never require that someone's blood must be shed before he is willing to forgive sin. Jesus told us to freely forgive multiple times with no sacrifice involved (see Matt 18:22). Why wouldn't God do the same?

These questions are important because the kind of God we worship determines the kind of people we will be. No one can be better than their God. Groups that imagine a violent, vengeful deity tend to become violent and vengeful. Groups that imagine a compassionate, forgiving deity tend to become compassionate and forgiving.

We see this illustrated every day around the world. Much terrorism, including cruelty and slaughter, is motivated by religion. Many say, "We love our god so much that we're obligated to kill anyone who doesn't." But Jesus's description of God is entirely different. He spent his life trying to correct erroneous concepts of God. He said, "Love your enemies and pray for those who persecute you, so that you may be children of your Father in heaven, for he makes his sun rise on the evil and on the good" (Matt 5:44–45).

He emphasized the fact that God is accepting and tolerant, saying, "Love your enemies, do good, and lend, expecting nothing in return. Your reward will be great, and you will be children of the Most High, for he himself is kind to the ungrateful and the wicked. Be merciful, just as your Father is merciful" (Luke 6:35–36).

Unscrupulous religious leaders use threats and warnings to manipulate people. They say, floods and famines and earthquakes and hurricanes are evidence of God's wrath, but Jesus said, it rains on the righteous and the unrighteous (see Matt 5:45).

Since we become like our object of worship, it's important for a commonsense gospel to acknowledge and eliminate these negative misconceptions about God.

The parable of the prodigal son is a wonderful description of how God treats his children. Jesus said,

> Then Jesus said, "There was a man who had two sons. The younger of them said to his father, 'Father, give me the share of the wealth that will belong to me.' So he divided his assets between them. A few days later the younger son gathered all he had and traveled to a distant region, and there he squandered his wealth in dissolute living. When he had spent everything, a severe famine took place throughout that region, and he began to be in need. So he went and hired himself out to one of the citizens of that region, who sent him to his fields to feed the pigs. He would gladly have filled his stomach with the pods that the pigs were eating, and no one gave him anything. But when he came to his senses he said, 'How

many of my father's hired hands have bread enough and to spare, but here I am dying of hunger! I will get up and go to my father, and I will say to him, "Father, I have sinned against heaven and before you; I am no longer worthy to be called your son; treat me like one of your hired hands."' So he set off and went to his father. But while he was still far off, his father saw him and was filled with compassion; he ran and put his arms around him and kissed him. Then the son said to him, 'Father, I have sinned against heaven and before you; I am no longer worthy to be called your son.' But the father said to his slaves, 'Quickly, bring out a robe—the best one—and put it on him; put a ring on his finger and sandals on his feet. And get the fatted calf and kill it, and let us eat and celebrate, for this son of mine was dead and is alive again; he was lost and is found!' And they began to celebrate." (Luke 15:11–24)

This story explains that we are children of God. It proves that forgiveness does not require payment or a substitutionary death. It shows that God loves us unconditionally. If we rebel or choose the wrong path, he gives us the freedom to fail and lets us suffer the consequences, but he still loves us. When we change our minds and come home again, he meets us halfway with joy and celebration.

It's important to note that this father required no sacrifice. He imposed no punishment. He even interrupted his son's apology. That's grace! That's how a real father would treat his child. That's the basis for a commonsense gospel!

In fact, Jesus constantly compares God to human parents, saying, "If the child asked for an egg, would give a scorpion?" (Luke 11:12).

He also said, "Is there anyone among you who, if your child asked for bread, would give a stone? Or if the child asked for a fish, would give a snake? If you, then, who are evil, know how to give good gifts to your children, how much more will your Father in heaven give good things to those who ask him!" (Matt 7:9–11).

A misguided religious leader recently said, "Man's slightest sin is an infinite offense to God and spiritually separates man from him and makes man God's enemy, deserving his wrath and eternal punishment." That's ridiculous!

One slight offense of a little boy or girl would not make that child an enemy of their earthly father. It would not make them deserve eternal punishment. Such a teaching is illogical, unbiblical, and dangerous. We must repudiate such beliefs and have faith in the God who is the father of Jesus Christ. Remember, Jesus said, "Whoever has seen me has seen the Father" (John 14:9).

Therefore, if Jesus wouldn't think, speak, or act in harsh and vengeful ways, then God doesn't do those things either! Jesus came to reveal the true God, and that's the one we must worship.

Religious individuals often discuss God's will. We especially label disastrous events as God's will. When insurance companies can't place blame for a tragedy, they call it an act of God. When we're reluctant to accept responsibility for an event, we pass the buck and make God the villain. When life is unfair and chaotic, we assume it's that way because God ordained it.

Once, parents who had lost a young son kept sobbing and repeating, "We have to realize that it's God's will!" This father had left out a box of rat poison, which the child had eaten and died. Yet all they could say was, "It's God's will!"

One speaker at a funeral said, "'We can't understand these things, but we know that God must have had a purpose for taking this baby." He was implying that God had deliberately caused great agony and suffering by taking an innocent life. That's not logical. It doesn't make sense!

Some may say, "But people derive comfort in time of sorrow by feeling that it's God's will." They may derive a little temporary comfort, but there can't be any lasting comfort in a falsehood. Only the truth can make us free.

A child in a casket is not God's will. When parents rear children in health and happiness, then we can say, "That's God's will." God doesn't bring about evil to produce good. God is good, and all that he does is good. James said, "Every generous act of giving, with every perfect gift, is from above, coming down from the Father of lights" (Jas 1:17).

Now, there is one sense in which God's will does apply. Consistent scientific principles are God's will. If a person falls off a cliff and is killed, that's not God's will. But it is God's will for the natural laws of gravity to operate on a regular basis. God is not being careless or unconcerned when he doesn't miraculously suspend one of these laws to save an individual's life.

God does care! His love for us is shown by his dependable laws. We would be puppets if God manipulated our actions. Our own initiative would be a farce if God overrode our choices by taking control of our cars, our bullets, and our behavior. When a child falls off his bike and breaks his arm, that doesn't mean his parents are unconcerned. It means the child was expressing his freedom. The parent will be the first to soothe the child and provide healing.

Even so, with God, what hurts his children hurts him, and he is the first to comfort us. But we can't keep our children from being hurt when they break natural laws, and God will not keep us from being hurt when we break natural laws.

If we label a tragedy as God's will, there is defeat. If we label it as a tragedy and let God help us overcome it, there is victory.

Maybe three brief analogies can help us understand something about God and how he operates.

Once, a governor, in his inaugural oath, swore to be honest in all state affairs. A few months later, a close friend asked for a special favor. He said, "You have a vacancy in one of your departments, and I really need the job. I'm not the best qualified or the most experienced applicant, but I'd appreciate it if you'd pull some strings on my behalf."

Can the honest governor grant that request? Of course he can't. It's not a matter of political clout or personal concern. The governor was powerful enough to do it. He could give the job, or he could remain an honest governor, but he couldn't do both! Some things are inherently incongruent.

Even God can't be a truthful liar.

A certain referee signed a contract promising that every call he made would be totally impartial. In a certain tournament, however, his own son was playing on a team. During the fourth quarter, the boy was about to foul out, so he said, "Dad, if you love me, you'll overlook my offense or change the rules just this once."

Can this impartial referee grant that request? Of course he can't. It's not a matter of urgency or fatherly love. He could overlook the offense, or he could operate as an impartial referee, but he couldn't do both. Some things are inherently incongruent.

Even God can't cheat fairly!

Once, a policeman was hired to protect individual human rights. In the course of his duties, he received many requests. One woman's thirty-year-old son joined a strange cult, and she wanted him arrested for his own good.

Can the freedom-granting policeman, who is committed to uphold individual human rights, grant that request? Of course he can't! It's not a matter of public good or private opinion. The policeman had the necessary strength and weapons to do this. He could use his position to satisfy an anxious mother, or he could respect individual autonomy, but he couldn't do both! Some things are inherently incongruent.

Even God can't create a free dictatorship.

In Jesus's parable of the talents, the master, who represents God, puts his agents, who represent us, in charge of affairs. He allows them to make their own decisions about investing the resources and then rewards those who are active and productive (see Matt 25:14–25).

Likewise, God has put us in charge of earthly affairs. The scripture says, "The heavens are the LORD's heavens, but the earth he has given to human beings" (Ps 115:16). God gave us unlimited resources, and he created us with infinite possibilities. He wants us to use those resources and take advantage of those possibilities. The religion that was being practiced in Jesus's day did not encourage or even allow people to be autonomous and responsible. For centuries men and women had believed they must adhere to senseless rules, perform complex rituals, and offer regular expressions of obeisance to keep a wrathful God satisfied and thus escape punishment.

Surprisingly, Jesus of Nazareth rejected many of the religious creeds and worship practices. He chose to proclaim a commonsense gospel. He redefined the erroneous ideas about God. He offered an individualized plan of salvation. He ignored many trivial rules and regulations. He even repudiated Old Testament teachings that were inhumane. He promised the gift of an internal guidance system called the Holy Spirit.

He taught and demonstrated a simple lifestyle based on only two principles: Love God, and love people (see Matt 22:36–40).

Jesus showed disdain for many of the traditional rules and regulations, saying, "Woe to you, scribes and Pharisees, hypocrites! For you tithe mint, dill, and cumin and have neglected the weightier matters of the law: justice and mercy and faith. It is these you ought to have practiced without neglecting the others. You blind guides! You strain out a gnat but swallow a camel!" (Matt 23:23–24).

Jesus broke rules about the Sabbath, saying, "The Sabbath was made for humankind and not humankind for the Sabbath" (Mark 2:27).

Jesus also refused to obey laws about stoning sinners. Once, the Pharisees brought a sinful woman and said, "Teacher, this woman was caught in the very act of committing adultery.... Moses commanded us to stone such women. Now what do you say?" Jesus answered, "Let anyone among you who is without sin be the first to throw a stone at her." After her accusers left, Jesus said to the woman, "Neither do I condemn you" (see John 8:3–11).

Jesus disregarded many of the customs and ceremonies, saying, "Whenever you pray, do not be like the hypocrites, for they love to stand and pray in the synagogues and at the street corners, so that they may be seen by others" (Matt 6:5).

He ridiculed their efforts to appear religious, saying, "They do all their deeds to be seen by others, for they make their phylacteries broad and their fringes long. They love to have the place of honor at banquets and the best seats in the synagogues and to be greeted with respect in the marketplaces and to have people call them rabbi" (Matt 23:5–7).

The religion that Jesus rejected was shallow and superficial. It dealt with irrelevant issues and emphasized many beliefs and practices that harmed innocent men and women. It portrayed a cruel deity who was more concerned with the rules of the law than with the pain of the people. Jesus realized that such a system was failing to meet the needs of individuals. He wanted to improve their lives.

When he viewed the multitudes, the scripture says, "He had compassion for them because they were harassed and helpless, like sheep without a shepherd" (Matt 9:36).

Jesus knew the people had a distorted perception of God. He wanted all human beings to have the same intimate relationship with God that he had. He believed it was his purpose to reveal the truth about God and to glorify God.

All of us need a father figure, a mentor, a hero, and an ideal to emulate. We need the God that Jesus called, "Abba, Father." Therefore, Jesus's commonsense gospel teaches that God is wise and loving.

Chapter 2:

Salvation Is Free and Reasonable

As parents try to keep their children safe and out of trouble, they often say and do things that make them feel guilty. When you scold a child and say, "No," they think that means, "There's something wrong with me!" or "I'm bad!" Little ones do need restraints and corrections, but their misunderstandings about these reprimands can create internal conflict and confusion. As a result, almost everyone grows up with self-doubts and defensive tendencies.

Because of this, most people reach adulthood feeling that they need some process to remove their flaws and absolve them of guilt. That's why a salvation experience has become the core theme of Christianity and an essential element of most religions.

Of course, each person has a different background, and each background produces specific problems. Therefore, personalized salvation is necessary. If the perversions and misconceptions have been caused by superstitious notions, then sometimes they may have to be corrected by dealing with those notions. If individuals believe they are depraved, subject to God's wrath and in danger of eternal punishment, they will be miserable. If they believe only the blood of a savior can cleanse them, then relying on the promise that Jesus's death did this for them will relieve their guilt and give them assurance. That's the reason Paul's belief in vicarious atonement was so important for him and so useful for his particular audience.

Nevertheless, this doctrine has two serious problems: First, it depicts God as a vengeful tyrant. Also, such a belief isn't reasonable or helpful to groups of people who have never been taught about sacrificial systems or threatened by literal descriptions of hell.

Christianity has greatly overemphasized the idea of sacrifice. To claim that a loving God demands the death and the shed blood of something or someone before he will offer forgiveness is ludicrous. Primitive groups got this notion of sacrifice because they believed their gods needed food and thus could be bribed. Remnants of that belief are found in the scriptures. One passage says, "Then Noah built an altar to the LORD and took of every clean animal and of every clean bird and offered burnt offerings on the altar. And when the LORD smelled the pleasing odor, the LORD said in his heart, 'I will never again curse the ground because of humans'" (Gen 8:20–21).

Even in the Old Testament a few deep thinkers began to recognize the problems with vicarious atonement. The psalmist ridiculed the claim that an omnipotent God needs sacrifices from us. He exclaimed that God isn't interested in sacrifices of bulls and goats. If he were hungry, he wouldn't ask people for food. The world and everything in it are his. He doesn't need sacrifices of flesh and blood. What he wants from us is gratitude and obedience (see Ps 50:8–14).

Samuel also questioned the matter, saying, "Has the LORD as great delight in burnt offerings and sacrifices as in obedience to the voice of the LORD? Surely, to obey is better than sacrifice and to heed than the fat of rams" (1 Sam 15:22).

David clearly said, "Sacrifice and offering you do not desire…. Burnt offering and sin offering you have not required" (Ps 40:6).

Isaiah explained that God rejected these practices and quotes him as saying, "What to me is the multitude of your sacrifices? says the Lord; I have had enough of burnt offerings of rams and the fat of fed beasts; I do not delight in the blood of bulls or of lambs or of goats" (Isa 1:11).

According to Jeremiah, God denied ever commanding a sacrificial system. He said, "In the day that I brought your ancestors out of the land of Egypt, I did not speak to them or command them concerning burnt offerings and sacrifices. But this command I gave them, 'Obey my voice, and I will be your God, and you shall be my people'" (Jer 7:22–23).

Several other prophets began to view sacrifices in a symbolic way and to associate morality with worship. The psalmist said, "Offer right sacrifices, and put your trust in the LORD" (Ps 4:5).

Hosea said, "I desire steadfast love and not sacrifice, the knowledge of God rather than burnt offerings" (Hos 6:6).

Micah goes further and defines God's requirements, saying, "Shall I come before him with burnt offerings, with calves a year old? Will the LORD be pleased with thousands of rams, with ten thousands of rivers of oil? Shall I give my firstborn for my transgression, the fruit of my body for the sin of my soul? He has told you, O mortal, what is good, and what does the LORD require of you but to do justice and to love kindness and to walk humbly with your God?" (see Mic 6:6–8).

Solomon agreed: "To do righteousness and justice is more acceptable to the LORD than sacrifice" (Prov 21:3).

Jesus simply said, "I desire mercy, not sacrifice" (Matt 9:13).

Once, he praised a man because he understood that God is more interested in love than sacrifice:

> Then the scribe said to him, "You are right, Teacher; you have truly said that 'he is one, and besides him there is no other'; and 'to love him with all the heart and with all the understanding and with all the strength' and 'to love one's neighbor as oneself'—this is much more important than all whole burnt offerings and sacrifices." When Jesus saw that he answered wisely, he said to him, "You are not far from the kingdom of God." After that no one dared to ask him any question. (Mark 12:32–34)

Paul, who more than anyone else seemed to emphasize the sacrificial system, also began to spiritualize the idea, saying, "I appeal to you therefore, brothers and sisters, on the basis of God's mercy, to present your bodies as a living sacrifice, holy and acceptable to God, which is your reasonable act of worship" (Rom 12:1).

The author of Hebrews described this new way of considering sacrifice, saying, "Through him, then, let us continually offer a sacrifice of praise to God, that is, the fruit of lips that confess his name. Do not neglect to do good and to share what you have, for such sacrifices are pleasing to God" (Heb 13:15–16).

Nevertheless, the idea of substitutionary sacrifice was still an ingrained belief of most Hebrews in the first century. Therefore, viewing Jesus's life and death from that perspective was a normal and helpful response. When John said, "In this is love, not that we loved God but that he loved us and sent his Son to be the atoning sacrifice for our sins" (1 John 4:10), this was true for him because he believed a payment for his sins was required. People today, however, have not had a background of belief in sacrifices, so they are not conditioned to understand or accept this strange interpretation.

As Christians we must get beyond pagan ideas and practices. We must reinterpret Jesus's death on the cross. His death was not necessary for God to forgive us; that would be a bribe. Our sins don't have to be paid for; that would be a transaction. Both common conversion explanations are illogical, because our basic teaching is that God's grace is free! The scripture says, "Grace…is the gift of God" (Eph 2:8). John the Baptist explained it this way: "From his fullness we have all received, grace upon grace. The law indeed was given through Moses; grace and truth came through Jesus Christ" (John 1:16–17).

Furthermore, Jesus clearly defined the purpose of his life and death. Just before his crucifixion he spoke to Pilate, saying, "For this I was born, and for this I came into the world, to testify to the truth" (John 18:37).

This truth, which Jesus came to express, includes the fact that we have a God of love, not wrath. We have a God who offers forgiveness, not vengeance. Jesus also expressed the truth about salvation, explaining that it's not based on the power of a blood sacrifice but rather on the love of God for his children. He taught us how to handle evil and how to forgive those who hurt us. Most of his parables encourage us to show concern for others and urge us to use our abilities and talents in productive ways.

We miss this essential information about Christian living when we only emphasize the death, burial, and resurrection. After all, Jesus is our model. He said, "I have set you an example, that you also should do as I have done to you" (John 13:15).

When Jesus said "believe in me," did he mean in him as an individual person, or did he mean in him as a representative of truth? This is a crucial question. It's a question that disturbs honest Christians. It's a question that divides religious denominations. It's a question that affects world relationships. It's a question with eternal significance.

Most evangelicals will immediately insist we must believe in Jesus as a particular historical character. But this requirement automatically excludes people who lived and died before Jesus was even born. It excludes those who happen to live in isolated cultures without any knowledge of the Judeo-Christian heritage. It excludes people who come from different backgrounds or use different expressions to describe their spiritual experiences. This is a serious issue, and regardless of what literalists say, exactly "what we are to believe" is not spelled out in the scriptures. Some verses do seem to emphasize belief in Jesus as an individual. John said, "Whoever believes in the Son has eternal life; whoever disobeys the Son will not see life" (John 3:36).

Other verses, however, point beyond Jesus to belief in God. Jesus said, "Anyone who hears my word and believes him who sent me has eternal life" (John 5:24).

He also says, "I can do nothing on my own. As I hear, I judge, and my judgment is just because I do not seek my own will but the will of him who sent me" (John 5:30).

Many verses, however, include the phrase *in his name:* "In his name the gentiles will hope" (Matt 12:21).

"To all who received him, who believed in his name, he gave power to become children of God" (John 1:12).

"These are written so that you may continue to believe that Jesus is the Messiah, the Son of God, and that through believing you may have life in his name" (John 20:31).

"There is no other name under heaven given among men by which we must be saved" (Acts 4:12).

This phrase may seem unimportant to us, but in the Greek language it is extremely important. The term *name* denotes the character, nature, or essence of something or someone.

Jesus himself sums it up this way, saying, "I am the way and the truth and the life. No one comes to the Father except through me" (John 14:6). He is really saying that his character, values, and teachings personify truth, and everyone must follow truth to have a productive life.

So the name of Jesus means the quality of his inner being, his personality traits, and the moral precepts he espoused. The concept of Christlikeness is suggested.

Then there are numerous verses that stress belief in valid moral principles. Jesus said to those Jews who believed in him, "If you continue in my word, you are truly my disciples" (John 8:31).

He also said, "You have already been cleansed by the word that I have spoken to you" (John 15:3).

Replacing fallacies with truth was the purpose of Jesus's message.

Several passages show that people believed and functioned as disciples without even knowing Jesus as a person. Once, Jesus heard the Pharisees had cast a person whom he had healed out of the synagogue. He found him and said, "'Do you believe in the Son of Man?' He answered, 'And who is he, sir? Tell me, so that I may believe in him.' Jesus said to him, 'You have seen him, and the one speaking with you is he'" (John 9:35–37).

All these verses prove that Jesus gave considerable leeway in regard to belief. He never advocated blind faith. Rather, he emphasized basing belief on evidence, saying, "If I am not doing the works of my Father, then do not believe me. But if I do them, even though you do not believe me, believe the works, so that you may know and understand that the Father is in me and I am in the Father" (John 10:37–38).

Jesus gives us two choices as to how we can believe, saying, "Believe me that I am in the Father and the Father is in me, but if you do not, then believe because of the works themselves" (John 14:11).

Understanding these deeper insights can help us resolve one of Christianity's greatest dilemmas: How can a just God condemn pagans or natives who have never had a chance to hear of Jesus? How can a just God condemn devout Jews, Christlike agnostics, and benevolent secularists who reflect Jesus's values? What about spiritual individuals like Gandhi? If souls like these populate hell, then it can't be entirely bankrupt!

Before we insist upon one narrow interpretation, let's remember that Jesus said,

"Each tree is known by its own fruit…. The good person out of the good treasure of the heart produces good" (Luke 6:44–45).

He also said, "A good tree cannot bear bad fruit, nor can a bad tree bear good fruit" (Matt 7:18). So if the fruit or the effects of a certain person's life or a particular group's contributions are obviously good, then we shouldn't judge and condemn them.

This is the point of Jesus's parable about the two sons. He said a father told his first son to go work in the vineyard. He answered and said, "I will not," but later he changed his mind and went. The father said the same thing to his second son. But he answered and said, "I will, sir," but then he did not go. When Jesus asked which of the two really did the will of his father, they said the first one (see Matt 21:28–31). In other words, Jesus is explaining that it's not our oral profession that determines our status; it's our actual performance.

Finally, let's remember that Jesus constantly linked himself with truth. He said, "You will know the truth, and the truth will make you free" (John 8:32). "When the Spirit of truth comes, he will guide you into all the truth" (John 16:13). "Everyone who belongs to the truth listens to my voice" (John 18:37).

When Jesus said "believe in me," did he mean in him as a person, or did he mean in him as a representative of spiritual truth? None of us know exactly what he meant!

Nevertheless, many scriptures indicate that if you follow truth and love people, then you do believe in the Christ, even if you don't use the traditional terminology.

The message Jesus brought to ordinary people was good news. His teachings and his acceptance of sinners threatened the arrogant religious leaders and the greedy power structures of this world. That's why he was crucified.

Jesus's teachings of love, forgiveness, productivity, and purpose still threaten people, but our world has changed. We have fewer authoritarian monarchs and superstitious teachings. Therefore, we must consider an entirely different salvation model. We know we were created in God's image (see Gen 1:27–28).

We also know little children are not born evil and depraved, because Jesus said everyone should become like a child to even see the kingdom of heaven (see Matt 18:3).

If children already have spiritual potential, then salvation has to be something that is realized rather than something that is received. For instance, flipping a light switch doesn't create electricity. It merely releases and activates something that is already there. Likewise, salvation releases and activates the spiritual possibilities that are already in an individual.

The requirements for salvation are different for each person. The gospel message for a man or woman is whatever frees them from ignorant superstition, senseless rules, and negative beliefs. It's whatever allows them to become aware of their true relationship with God. That's why salvation must be individualized.

During the Civil War, a widower with small children was drafted, but his single neighbor volunteered to go in his place and was killed. When the news came, the father searched until he found the body of his substitute. He buried it in the church yard and chiseled this epitaph on the tombstone: "He died for me!"

For some people salvation must be stated in exactly these terms. For others the understanding may be very different. Whatever it takes to make a person whole and productive is that person's salvation.

God doesn't have a list of rules we must obey or a list of requirements we must meet. He accepts us as we are and offers grace.

It's our own realization of this great blessing and our own belief that God does love and accept us as we are that verifies our salvation experience. When Jesus helped a seeker, he never said, "My power has done this for you." He invariably declared, "Your faith has made you whole."

Many real-life situations operate this way. If you were a convicted criminal awaiting execution and the governor signed your pardon, you wouldn't feel any relief and joy if you didn't know you had been pardoned or if you didn't believe you had been pardoned. It's not the fact of the pardon that produces the results. It's your realization of the pardon and your belief in the pardon that causes the changes in you.

Martin Luther was right when he said, "If religion is to be efficacious, it must be transmitted in personal pronouns. It is for me!" That's the only statement that's important.

Salvation was a basic theme and purpose of Jesus's mission. He said, "The Son of Man came to seek out and to save the lost" (Luke 19:10). Being lost, however, doesn't mean being evil. It means being separated, estranged, and confused.

The conversion experience enables human beings to realize their relationship to God and enter his kingdom, but it's often misunderstood. Many people view it as an instantaneous event that changes sinners into saints the moment they comply with a simple three-step formula of repent, believe, and commit. Unfortunately, these converts are rarely given any explanation about the reasons for such a transformation. They aren't told the dramatic change is in them, not in God. They don't understand it's the fulfillment of their own needs for acceptance and love that helps them become autonomous, confident, and productive. Then it's the assurance of their status that gives them a sense of security and purpose. This is what allows them to live an abundant life.

Jesus gave a clear explanation of salvation in several parables. He said,

> All the nations will be gathered before him, and he will separate people one from another as a shepherd separates the sheep from the goats, and he will put the sheep at his right hand and the goats at the left. Then the king will say to those at his right hand, "Come, you who are blessed by my Father, inherit the kingdom prepared for you from the foundation of the world, for I was hungry and you gave me food, I was thirsty and you gave me something to drink, I was a stranger and you welcomed me, I was naked and you gave me clothing, I was sick and you took care of me, I was in prison and you visited me." Then the righteous will answer him, "Lord, when

was it that we saw you hungry and gave you food or thirsty and gave you something to drink? And when was it that we saw you a stranger and welcomed you or naked and gave you clothing? And when was it that we saw you sick or in prison and visited you?" And the king will answer them, "Truly I tell you, just as you did it to one of the least of these brothers and sisters of mine, you did it to me." Then he will say to those at his left hand, "You who are accursed, depart from me into the eternal fire prepared for the devil and his angels, for I was hungry and you gave me no food, I was thirsty and you gave me nothing to drink, I was a stranger and you did not welcome me, naked and you did not give me clothing, sick and in prison and you did not visit me." Then they also will answer, "Lord, when was it that we saw you hungry or thirsty or a stranger or naked or sick or in prison and did not take care of you?" Then he will answer them, "Truly I tell you, just as you did not do it to one of the least of these, you did not do it to me." (Matt 25:32–46)

These goats had demonstrated by their inaction that the Christ Spirit was not within them.

According to this analogy, neither the sheep nor the goats were personally acquainted with Jesus. They had never knowingly interacted with him.

Jesus may have been referring to people like these righteous ones when he said, "I have other sheep that do not belong to this fold. I must bring them also, and they will listen to my voice. So there will be one flock, one shepherd" (John 10:16).

Jesus explained that showing concern and love for even the least of these other people is the same as showing concern and love for him and for God. This parable provides strong evidence that believing in Jesus's name means to identify with his nature, his character, and his values, not necessarily with him as an individual.

Sometimes problems and misunderstandings arise because people tend to interpret everything on a strictly either/or basis. Children learn a vocabulary of opposite words before almost anything else. If you say "up," they say "down." If you say "hot," they say "cold." If you say "good," they say, "bad." This thinking pattern originated in ancient populations. When it developed, it had a purpose and filled a vital need. Exclusiveness was once pro-survival. Labeling my group as right and superior and labeling all other groups as wrong and inferior gave groups confidence and cohesiveness. This sense of unity helped vulnerable tribes in their struggle against enemies. This "us against them" mentality was probably necessary in a primitive society. But as civilization progressed, it has become less beneficial. In today's global society, with a wide range of beliefs and lifestyles, it has become detrimental and even dangerous.

In a small world, with many diverse cultures, intolerance leads to prejudice, discrimination, and even war. Our exclusive religion has forced us to compartmentalize, and that creates hostility. In our daily life we interact with people of many different cultures and faiths. It's impossible to respect and honor these fellow citizens if you must regard them as pagans and enemies.

People who accept a commonsense gospel agree with evangelical Christians that Jesus did die for us. But they believe he died to proclaim and preserve truth, not to pay for our sins or to appease an angry God.

All honest seekers come to know God by this same truth that Jesus exemplified. An old proverb says it well: "Lamps are different; light is the same."

Since God is just and Jesus was compassionate, we know neither of them would demand unreasonable responses.

There was no worldwide evangelism in those early centuries, so belief in a particular person known as Jesus Christ would have been impossible. Multitudes of Asians, North Americans, Africans, and others who lived and died before communication and transportation were available would never have had a chance to believe.

Perhaps Helen Keller, who was blind and deaf, explained it best. When she finally understood about God, she replied, "Oh, I knew him. I just didn't know his name."

Once, in describing their mission, the scripture says, "[The disciples] went through the villages, bringing the good news" (Luke 9:6).

When these men went out preaching the gospel, they knew nothing of the death, burial, and resurrection of Jesus. None of this had happened. They couldn't preach about the cross or the vicarious atonement, and these are the things that constitute the gospel message for most Christians.

So what did these disciples preach? Well, the word *gospel* means "good news," and Jesus brought the good news of God's love and acceptance. He emphasized our worth as God's children and our purpose as God's agents here on earth.

Jesus said, "You are of more value than many sparrows" (Matt 10:31).

A belief that God accepts and values us as we are was Zacchaeus's gospel. When Jesus offered to have fellowship with him in his home, that validated his worth as a person and enabled him to change his behavior. Jesus said, "'Zacchaeus, hurry and come down, for I must stay at your house today.' So he hurried down and was happy to welcome him" (Luke 19:5–6).

Jesus also brought the good news of forgiveness and reassurance. The woman at the well needed forgiveness and hope. She had a load of guilt and regret (see John 4:10–14). A belief that we can solve our problems, leave our past behind, and begin to enjoy a worthwhile life gives us security and peace.

Then the gospel motivates us and defines our purpose. That's good news! Jesus said, "If you love me, you will keep my commandments" (John 14:15).

A belief that we are to act on our faith was James's gospel. It motivated him to witness and serve. He said, "Show me your faith apart from works, and I by my works will show you faith" (Jas 2:18).

Each of these individuals responded to the specific aspect of spirituality that was meaningful to them. Whatever people need to understand to change and grow and reach their potential is their gospel!

Later, Paul desperately needed freedom, so a belief that Jesus paid for our sins once and for all was Paul's gospel. It liberated him from the terrible burden of temple sacrifices. It liberated him from the awful guilt of breaking numerous Pharisaical laws. It liberated him from the paralyzing fear of a wrathful God. He expressed his sense of liberation when he said, "The law of the Spirit of life in Christ Jesus has set you free from the law of sin and of death" (Rom 8:2).

Individuals are at different stages of maturity, and because of their unique temperaments, backgrounds, and experiences, different people need different things.

In the maturing process we move one step at a time. That's why the sacrificial rituals and atonement theories that were developed and practiced over the years may have been helpful and even necessary for primitive people. Ceremonies such as kneeling at altars, lighting candles, counting rosary beads, being baptized, and observing Communion have become essential elements in many people's religion. As a result of this conditioning, some men and women may have to do whatever their own traditions have taught them to do to make them feel forgiven and secure.

If we need to repeat certain words, then we should say them! If we need to perform certain procedures, then we should do them! But we should not claim it is God who requires all these observances, and we should not demand that everyone else must say and do these same things to be accepted.

Some evangelists insist salvation is achieved by agreeing to a brief formula. But if there is one exact way to move a person from an unsaved to a saved position, then why didn't Jesus repeat that magic formula to everyone he met? If going through a quick and easy process can change a sinner into a saint, then why didn't Jesus ask each of his followers to complete that process? If a particular repentance, belief, and commitment procedure is required before a soul is converted, then why didn't Jesus make that the theme of every sermon he preached?

When we honestly examine Jesus's own witnessing techniques, we find he never offered one formula or process or procedure that everybody could follow to achieve salvation. He always evaluated each individual and expressed his recommendations in ways to meet that person's specific needs.

To Jesus, salvation was not a ticket to heaven. He viewed salvation as a realization or an experience that heals people from their past injuries and pain. This in turn delivers them from their negative feelings of guilt and regret. It also removes their desires for retribution and vengeance. Eliminating these psychological hindrances enables these fortunate individuals to enjoy an abundant life now and for eternity. With James and John, Jesus said, "Leave your occupation and follow me." With the woman at the well, he questioned her relationship problems and said, "Let me quench your thirst with living water." With the rich young ruler, he asked about his moral code and then told him to get rid of his wealth. With one crowd he insisted they should become childlike. With Nicodemus, who already considered himself morally acceptable because he had the correct birth lineage back to Abraham, Jesus advised starting all over by being born from above.

Jesus counseled Samaritans, Syro-Phoenicians, and Roman centurions, yet he never commanded any of them to immediately abandon all their own religious beliefs and traditions.

Salvation means attaining wholeness. This may happen gradually through a learning and maturing process, or it can happen suddenly if an enlightening event or insight occurs. Jesus helps each person reach that state, not to satisfy a vindictive God but rather to assure them of having a successful and productive life!

Sometimes Jesus gives us a clue that is overlooked. In his final message to us he says, "Go therefore and make disciples of all nations… teaching them to obey everything that I have commanded you" (Matt 28:19–20).

All of us have heard this great commission, but we may have missed one important word: He said, "Teach them what I have taught you," not what Moses taught you, or what Paul is going to teach you, or what some religious group is determined to teach you. In other words, we must base our doctrines on Jesus's teachings. We should emphasize what he emphasized. Churches today don't always do that.

John also wrote a scripture passage in which one word totally reinterprets the gospel message. He said, "Everyone who loves is born of God and knows God" (1 John 4:7).

He didn't say every Christian who loves, or every believer who loves, or every church member who loves. He said everyone who loves! Does this mean those Buddhists, Muslims, Jews, and agnostics who truly love and show that love to their families, friends, and neighbors are born of God and know God?

That's exactly what this Bible verse says, and the next verse goes even further, stating the negative version of this concept, saying, "Whoever does not love does not know God, for God is love" (1 John 4:8).

It seems love has been greatly underrated as an element of salvation. Peter said, "Above all, maintain constant love for one another, for love covers a multitude of sins" (1 Peter 4:8). Jesus said the same thing about the prostitute who washed his feet. When the Pharisees criticized him for allowing such a sinner to touch him, he said, "Her many sins have been forgiven.... She has shown great love" (Luke 7:47–48).

The word *love* doesn't mean to be romantic or even to be affectionate. In the Greek language this term is *agape*, which means to be genuinely concerned about the welfare of someone. To illustrate this basic value, Jesus told a story about an injured man who was ignored by several people before he was aided by an unusual benefactor. He said, "A Samaritan while traveling came upon him, and when he saw him he was moved with compassion" (Luke 10:33).

We call him the good Samaritan. Now why is this Samaritan called good? Is he good because of who he was? Not at all! The Samaritans were a despised race of renegades and half-breeds, and Jesus didn't even mention his lineage or his social status.

Was he good because of what he believed? Not at all! The Samaritans were a heretical, unorthodox religious group, and Jesus didn't even mention his creed or his religious faith.

Was he good because of his high moral code? Not at all! The Samaritans were considered to be wrong on many matters of law keeping, and Jesus didn't even mention his morals or his character.

Why, then, was he called good? Well, he was praised for one thing and one thing only. He had concern for other people!

The story Jesus told about two groups called sheep and goats, who came before the great judge and received unexpected verdicts, teach this same lesson. They were also praised for one thing and one thing only: They had shown concern for others.

Jesus never discussed depravity, vicarious atonement, or propitiation for sin. In fact, he seldom mentioned sin at all. He advised his followers to ignore the tares or weeds, telling them that attacking sinners and crusading against evil often does more harm than good.

If you carefully study the teachings of Jesus, you'll find he only required two things: Love God, and love people.

On the other hand, he mainly criticized and condemned two things: hypocrisy and unconcern.

So seekers who decide to follow Jesus must promise to love God and love people.

They must promise to be honest and real, not deceitful and hypocritical.

They must promise to be generous and productive, not greedy and unconcerned.

These are the traits that can be found in the lives of individuals who have had a true and permanent conversion. These are the traits that describe the fruits or effects of a free and reasonable salvation experience.

It's unfortunate that Christian groups often have irreconcilable differences about this matter of salvation.

Some predestinarians believe certain elect ones are called of God and all others are condemned to perdition. A few scriptures do seem to support this extreme doctrine. Jesus said, "For the sake of the elect, whom he chose, he has cut short those days" (Mark 13:20).

Another verse says, "As many as had been destined for eternal life became believers" (Acts 13:48).

Paul said, "God chose you as the first fruits for salvation" (2 Thess 2:13).

This doctrine of predestination is so blatantly unfair that not many groups still preach it.

Then most evangelicals teach that everyone has the possibility of salvation, but it's only those who recognize their lost condition, repent of their sins, and trust Jesus's death, burial, and resurrection for their redemption who are saved. Those who don't hear the gospel, or else hear it and neglect it or understand it differently, remain lost.

People who hold this view concerning salvation believe human beings in their natural state are creations of God, but not children of God. They believe Adam and Eve's sin, which led to the fall, caused all humanity to be depraved. Therefore, each person must be restored to a divine relationship by personally accepting Christ's atonement.

The Philippian jailer asked, "'Sirs, what must I do to be saved?' [Paul and Silas] answered, 'Believe in the Lord Jesus, and you will be saved, you and your household'" (Acts 16:30–31).

Paul also said, "If you confess with your mouth that Jesus is Lord and believe in your heart that God raised him from the dead, you will be saved" (Rom 10:9).

Christians who accept a commonsense gospel are different. They view all human beings as potential sons and daughters of the heavenly Father. They explain that it's the realization and actualization of their true status that gives them the benefits of salvation.

There are several important scriptures that do support and explain this universal salvation doctrine. Paul alludes to this idea, saying, "The grace of God has appeared, bringing salvation to all" (Titus 2:11).

Then he says, "One man's act of righteousness leads to justification and life for all" (Rom 5:18).

He also said, "For as all die in Adam, so all will be made alive in Christ" (1 Cor 15:22).

The scripture says, "All flesh shall see the salvation of God" (Luke 3:6).

It also says, "He is the atoning sacrifice for our sins, and not for ours only but also for the sins of the whole world" (1 John 2:2).

The parable of the prodigal son clearly shows this boy's relationship to his father was never in question. The father, who represents God, declares, "This son of mine was dead and is alive again" (Luke 15:24).

This young man was his father's son before he left! He was his father's son while he was gone! He was his father's son after he came home! His physical safety, comfort, and productivity were jeopardized while he was away, but his relationship to his father was never in doubt! He was always his father's son! This indicates that forgiveness is the permanent attitude of God toward us, not a special reaction triggered by our repentance. John the Baptist said, "Here is the Lamb of God who takes away the sin of the world!" (John 1:29).

The thief on the cross was a criminal who had been convicted of some terrible offense. He admitted he was guilty. Yet he didn't do anything to get right. He merely said, "Remember me" (see Luke 23:40–42).

Jesus didn't say, "Have you repented of your sins? Do you believe God sent me to die for you? Do you believe I'll rise again? Do you accept me as your personal savior?" He didn't say, "Have you been baptized? Have you made a public profession of faith? Have you joined a church?" He didn't even say, "Have you been born again?" He simply said, "Truly I tell you, today you will be with me in paradise" (Luke 23:43).

Many parallels from real life verify this description of salvation. A farmer can own land with valuable oil for decades without knowing about it or profiting from it. The pump doesn't add wealth to the property; it merely makes available the wealth that was already there.

Once, a merchant sold what he thought was a pretty rock. Later, the lucky buyer discovered it was a sapphire worth a lot of money. Now, did that rock miraculously turn into an expensive jewel at some point? No, of course not! It was a sapphire all the time. But it was not valuable to the first guy who had it. It was only valuable to the guy who had it and knew he had it.

A simple story may clarify these three views of salvation. Three families moved into newly constructed homes. When winter came, each family was cold, and each family called their contractor to complain.

The first contractor said, "I'm sorry, but you weren't one of those chosen to receive a furnace. You'll have to freeze." This represents a predestination view of salvation. It's something provided by God for a few elect ones.

The second contractor said, "Okay, since you've recognized your plight and asked me for help, I'll give you a furnace." This represents the evangelical view of salvation. It's something available to all, but only those individuals who ask for it get it.

The third contractor said, "The furnace was built in. I've already anticipated and met all your needs. Just turn it on and enjoy it." This represents a universal view of salvation. It's already provided to everyone. We are entitled to benefit from it and enjoy it. That's why believing is so important. You have to believe you are God's child and behave as God's child before you can enjoy the benefits of being God's child.

The story of the ugly duckling also illustrates this point. We often say, "And then the ugly duckling became a beautiful swan." That's false! This bird was a swan all the time. Before he was hatched, he was a swan. When he was being ridiculed by the ducks, he was a swan. When he was being persecuted by the animals, he was a swan! He just didn't know he was a swan! He believed what others had told him and therefore thought he was an ugly duckling and behaved like an ugly duckling. It was only when he realized it was his basic nature to be a swan that he was able to benefit from it and behave like it! That's salvation!

To Jesus, salvation means knowing your real worth and achieving your real purpose. This leads to a practical, productive, compassionate lifestyle. It's a gospel normal people can understand and believe in.

All of us need to know we belong to God's family. We need feelings of acceptance, love, forgiveness, value, security, purpose, and hope. Therefore, Jesus's commonsense gospel teaches that salvation is free and reasonable.

Chapter 3:

Doctrines Must Be Positive and Realistic

The gospel that's being preached today includes several negative doctrines and beliefs that need to be modified or updated. It has too many obsolete rules and unnecessary requirements. If taken literally, there are some scriptures that can be used to support slavery, torture, child abuse, racial injustice, gender bias, and other questionable practices.

Jesus repudiated or ignored those unproductive and harmful passages. His messages were always positive and helpful. Once, he told a story that explained how to handle evil:

> The kingdom of heaven may be compared to someone who sowed good seed in his field, but while everybody was asleep an enemy came and sowed weeds among the wheat and then went away. So when the plants came up and bore grain, then the weeds appeared as well. And the slaves of the householder came and said to him, "Master, did you not sow good seed in your field? Where, then, did these weeds come from?" He answered, "An enemy has done this." The slaves said to him, "Then do you want us to go and gather them?" But he replied, "No, for in gathering the weeds you would uproot the wheat along with them. Let both of them grow together until

the harvest, and at harvest time I will tell the reapers, Collect the weeds first and bind them in bundles to be burned, but gather the wheat into my barn." (Matt 13:24–30)

Jesus knew overzealous moralists can do more damage than sinners. If he were here today, he wouldn't waste his time attacking evil. He wouldn't constantly criticize behavior. He wouldn't condemn specific sins. He wouldn't lead anti-crime crusades. He wouldn't carry signs promoting abstinence. Instead, he would agree with what Paul later advised and seek to "overcome evil with good" (Rom 12:21).

It's significant that Jesus rarely judged, threatened, or punished sinners. He defended a prostitute who washed his feet. He disobeyed Moses's rules and even Old Testament commandments by refusing to condemn an adulteress. When the Pharisees quoted scripture to prove she should be stoned, he replied wisely: "Let anyone among you who is without sin be the first to throw a stone at her" (John 8:7).

If Jesus were here now, his sermons would not be of the fire-and-brimstone variety. It's more likely he would be having coffee with non-Christians and socializing with those who are considered unacceptable in polite society. He even told the orthodox, law-abiding Jews that the tax-gatherers and prostitutes would enter the kingdom of God ahead of them (see Matt 21:31).

Most people don't realize that when Jesus said this, he was talking to the chief priests and elders. These were the highly respected religious leaders who obeyed every commandment and believed every traditional doctrine. He was also comparing them to publicans who were unpatriotic traitors and thieves and to harlots who were immoral prostitutes and adulteresses. Now, Jesus wasn't condoning the sins of theft and promiscuity. Rather, he was pointing out that this class of sinners was more likely to repent than the "holier than thou" group of hypocrites. Also, he was evaluating the relative long-term damage of their behavior. He realized that, overall, the judgmental attitudes and hypocritical lifestyles of the Pharisees were more destructive to ordinary people and a greater hindrance to spiritual progress than the financial and sexual sins of publicans and prostitutes.

Sometimes modern Christians have questions about obeying the many rules and regulations of their religion, but Jesus dealt with this situation. When his disciples picked and ate grain on the Sabbath, critics were quick to attack. Jesus used an Old Testament incident to prove that disobedience can sometimes be the better choice in emergencies: "He said to them, 'Have you never read what David did when he and his companions were hungry and in need of food, how he entered the house of God when Abiathar was high priest and ate the bread of the Presence, which it is not lawful for any but the priests to eat, and he gave some to his companions?'" (Mark 2:25–26).

Jesus even justified breaking religious commandments. Once, when he met a man with a withered hand on the Sabbath day, his critics asked him, "'Is it lawful to cure on the Sabbath?' so that they might accuse him. He said to them, 'Suppose one of you has only one sheep and it falls into a pit on the Sabbath; will you not lay hold of it and lift it out? How much more valuable is a human being than a sheep! So it is lawful to do good on the Sabbath'" (Matt 12:10–12). If nurses or firemen are required to work on Sunday, they can be sure that Jesus understands why they missed church to help sick or injured people.

The eternal punishment of hell is another confusing issue that is often misunderstood. Again, the scriptures give very little specific information about this subject. The traditional description of hell is physically dangerous, intellectually illogical, and spiritually reprehensible.

This doctrine is physically dangerous because it encourages intolerance, revenge, and cruelty. In a diverse society we must work and live with men and woman of various religions. We can't extend sincere justice and love to people who we believe are destined to eternal damnation. If God imposes that kind of vicious penalty on these people, then we will feel free to condemn and scorn them.

The doctrine of hell is intellectually illogical because it has no redemptive purpose. It doesn't discipline or rehabilitate. It only inflicts pain. Unless punishment causes us to learn from our mistakes or change our behavior, it becomes nothing more than vengeance.

The doctrine of hell is spiritually reprehensible because it portrays a merciless God of wrath. Why would a loving creator set up such a sadistic and useless system? Think about it: In civilized countries today, torture is not allowed even for ruthless traitors and murderous criminals. Our law forbids the use of cruel and unusual punishment. Are we, as sinful human beings, more humane than God?

Jesus did say, "If your right eye causes you to sin, tear it out and throw it away; it is better for you to lose one of your members than for your whole body to be thrown into hell" (Matt 5:29). But nobody interprets that literally! Jesus did say, "Do not fear those who kill the body but cannot kill the soul; rather, fear the one who can destroy both soul and body in hell" (Matt 10:28). But the word *destroy* means to utterly abolish or eliminate. It doesn't mean to inflict pain and anguish on living beings forever.

Jesus attacked one group, saying, "You snakes, you brood of vipers! How can you escape the judgment of hell?" (Matt 23:33). But this word we've translated as *hell* or *hades* refers to Gehenna, which was a public garbage pit outside Jerusalem where worthless things were being reduced to ashes. This conflagration certainly didn't keep people or even trash intact in the flames. Jesus was really saying, "If you live an evil and useless life, you can't escape ending up on the garbage heap."

Jesus told a parable about the rich man in hell and Lazarus the beggar, but parables are analogies that teach one lesson, and the lesson in that case was to point out the danger of unconcern and neglect, not to describe a method of punishment (see Luke 16:24–25).

Peter mentioned hell, but he described it as a strange dark pit that was a holding place for disobedient angels before judgment day: "God did not spare the angels when they sinned but cast them into hell and committed them to chains of deepest darkness to be kept until the judgment" (2 Peter 2:4).

Several times hell is called *outer darkness* (see Matt 22:13; 25:30). These varying descriptions send conflicting messages about a literal hell.

If hell is a place where evil people and evil spirits and vengeance and hatred will continue to exist forever, then good doesn't really triumph, and God can never be totally victorious. Yet the scripture says, "Then I saw a new heaven and a new earth…. God himself will be with them…. He will wipe every tear from their eyes. Death will be no more; mourning and crying and pain will be no more" (Rev 21:1, 3–4). Paul also said that in the end God will be all in all (see 1 Cor 15:27–28).

In general, religion has always been too negative. Once, Christians denounced movies until TV forced their hand. Then dancing was a favorite taboo until culture modified their attitudes. Every time moralists paint themselves into a corner and have to recant, their credibility is weakened. We must be able to separate the truth of God from the normal activities and inevitable developments of society.

Negative doctrines impede progress. Some groups even practice closed Communion. This judgmental practice prohibits Christians of different belief systems from sharing in the Lord's Supper. It's a rule that is based on tradition, not scripture! It's based on exclusiveness, not love! It's based on hypocrisy, not honesty!

There are no specific biblical or New Testament guidelines on open or closed Communion because there were no different denominations at that time. However, the churches were as varied in beliefs and practices as different denominations are today. Jerusalem was nothing like Corinth. There were controversies and divisions concerning eating meat, speaking in tongues, and requiring circumcision. Even so, there is no indication that Paul and Peter were prohibited from breaking bread together because they disagreed on certain issues.

The doctrine of closed Communion is radically opposed to everything Jesus stood for! It rejects and alienates. It causes hurts and misunderstandings.

A successful man declared that he'd had no respect for religion since childhood because he'd seen a sweet old lady being snubbed when the Lord's Supper was being served. She attended and supported a local church because there was no church of her denomination available yet was made to feel unwelcome at the Lord's table.

Stories like this are common! Intelligent, sensitive people are turned off by such hurtful regulations.

Jesus said all doctrines and practices must be evaluated by their fruits! Things must be judged by their effects, their consequences, and their results. Absolutely no good fruit ever comes from this doctrine. We never hear a person say, "The doctrine of closed Communion has enriched my life, made me more loving, or made this a better world!" On the contrary, it invariably has the exact opposite effect!

Furthermore, this rule is hypocritical. Associations and conventions that have such doctrinal requirements in their constitutions are at best guilty of grossly misplaced priorities. Churches can be full of hatred, prejudice, and greed; they can neglect outreach and ministry; they can have a history of conflicts and divisions and yet be in good standing. But if they allow Christians from other groups to join them in sharing the Lord's Supper, they are disfellowshipped.

Another strange exclusionary doctrine sometimes called *alien immersion* is also a hindrance to unity. Some churches will not accept people who have been baptized in other denominations. They insist upon rebaptizing them. Such judgmental positions are not Christlike.

Why do groups pick trivial legalities like these as their ultimate tests of fellowship? Surely there are weightier matters to consider!

A woman's role in society is another problematic issue among Christians. Jesus always elevated the status of women. In his interesting encounter with the Greek woman, she argued that even the dogs are allowed to eat the children's crumbs. For a woman and a foreigner to speak so boldly to a man was astonishing, but his response shows us that he wasn't a male chauvinist. Rather than requiring submissive behavior from a female, he was intrigued and amused by her show of wit and determination.

The controversy concerning women in the ministry has been detrimental in the spread of the Christian gospel. This subject must be studied in the total context of Jesus's teachings. The spirit, not the letter, must be considered. Jesus worked within the cultural framework of his times, but the whole theme, and the very heart of his message, elevated the worth and dignity of every individual!

Even the Apostle Paul admitted that in God's kingdom, "There is no longer male and female" (Gal 3:28).

Peter assures us, "God shows no partiality" (Acts 10:34).

If women are looked upon as less worthy or competent, then the door is immediately opened to all the things Jesus hated most—racism, bigotry, and discrimination. Our Lord showed repeatedly that individuals are equal. In his daring defense of the woman taken in adultery, he opposed the tragic evils of a society that condones double standards. An incident with Martha gives us some vital information about Jesus's opinion. She came to him and said, "Lord, do you not care that my sister has left me to do all the work by myself? Tell her, then, to help me.' But the Lord answered her, 'Martha, Martha, you are worried and distracted by many things, but few things are needed—indeed only one. Mary has chosen the better part, which will not be taken away from her'" (Luke 10:40–42).

This shows us exactly how Jesus would treat a modern woman who chooses to study theology or do scientific research instead of being a proper housewife! When he approved Mary's desire for the intellectual involvement that was usually reserved for men, while Martha carried out a woman's role in the kitchen, he was strongly protecting each person's right to serve God in his or her own way.

In the early church, the social opinions and culture of the times influenced customs. Women and other groups—such as Samaritans, Gentiles, and slaves—had little respect and few privileges. On the subject of human rights, Jesus clearly presented the principles of the worth and dignity of all individuals and expected steady growth in that area. It's unfortunate that after two thousand years, the church, whose very mission is to elevate the value of people, still lags behind government, industry, entertainment, and even sports in this crucial matter.

When he wrote to Timothy, Paul said, "I do not permit a woman to teach or to have authority over a man; she is to keep silent" (1 Tim 2:12). But then in his letter to the church in Corinth, he gave contradictory advice when he said women should keep silent in the church (see 1 Cor 14:34). In that same letter, however, he described how women should be dressed when they do pray or preach, saying, "Any woman who prays or prophesies with her head unveiled shames her head" (1 Cor 11:5). This clearly indicates that customs varied. Paul was not giving a universal prohibition; he was simply trying to handle a specific local situation.

In fact, many women held leadership positions in the first century. Anna was a respected prophet who blessed Jesus when he was a baby (see Luke 2:36). A prophet is one who speaks for God or gives God's message to the people. A woman glorified God in the synagogue in Jesus's presence, and he didn't tell her to be quiet (see Luke 13:10–13). The woman at the well proclaimed the gospel to a whole city (see John

4:28–29). Jesus personally sent out women with a verbal message to men announcing his resurrection (see Matt 28:10).

Phoebe was a church leader (see Rom 16:1–5). Lydia seemed to be in a place of authority (see Acts 16:13–15). And Phillip's four daughters had the gift of prophecy (see Acts 21:9).

Apollos was definitely taught by Priscilla (see Acts 18:24–26). At Pentecost all the people spoke. This included many women (see Acts 1:14; 2:1–18).

Both Joel and Peter also foretell that in the future both men and women will proclaim the gospel. The scripture says, "In the last days it will be, God declares, that I will pour out my Spirit upon all flesh, and your sons and your daughters shall prophesy" (Acts 2:17).

Taken in their entirety, the scriptures indicate that both men and women are to fill needs as they occur.

When a woman did an unusual and inappropriate thing by anointing his feet with a costly perfume, Jesus said, "Leave her alone" (John 12:7).

In our world today there is a need for ministers in the military, penitentiaries, hospitals, and churches. Why do we create hindrances for half our population? The sharply delineated role of pastor/layman is inevitably fading as various ministries are developing in the areas of administration, youth, senior citizens, and counseling. Preaching is even being done by puppets and animated characters. Which of these are we going to designate as a men-only category?

Imagine what Jesus would say: "Oh, you blind guides, have you nothing better to do in these perilous times than to prohibit the proclamation of the gospel by willing volunteers?"

For Christians, making moral choices can be disturbing and difficult. Of course, there are a few universal principles that must remain absolute! Actions that harm people or property or nature are wrong. But many other specific things are not absolute. The morality or immorality of most things must be determined by their association and their situation.

Over the years Christians have changed their beliefs and behavior about a lot of trivial matters such as makeup, hairstyles, playing cards, and having ball games on Sunday. Today, trying to place absolute right or wrong labels on every single issue is not working. For instance, we can't emphasize responsible drinking if we must demand total abstinence. Young people are intelligent enough to know that sipping a little champagne at weddings is not the same as drunk driving. They realize it's not alcohol that's evil; it's the use of it.

Absolutism doesn't allow for any choices of better and worse alternatives. It doesn't analyze or consider motives or context. It doesn't admit that some things are all right occasionally but not all the time; that some things are all right in moderation but not when carried to extremes; that some things are all right under certain conditions but not others.

We already apply this non-absolute moral standard to determine the sin of gluttony. We don't require total fasting or starvation. We just say be sensible and moderate. We must learn how to do this with a lot of other things too. Fortunately, we have scriptural guidelines to follow. In the Bible, the question of eating meat offered to idols is comparable to some issues today. Paul dealt with it by adapting his behavior to different groups. He says that if he's in a culture that accepts this practice, he goes along, but if he's in a culture that would be offended, he abstains (see 1 Cor 8:7–13).

He went even further about personal moral choices, saying, "Those who eat must not despise those who abstain, and those who abstain must not pass judgment on those who eat, for God has welcomed them. Who are you to pass judgment on slaves of another? It is before their own lord that they stand or fall. And they will be upheld, for the Lord is able to make them stand.

Some judge one day to be better than another, while others judge all days to be alike. Let all be fully convinced in their own minds" (Rom 14:3–5).

A commonsense gospel should not include lists of specific opinions with labels as to whether they are absolutely right or wrong. It should not include lists of specific actions with labels as to whether they are absolutely good or evil. Very few things can be so easily designated. It's important to note that Jesus didn't mandate any rules concerning a person's choices about food, clothing, recreation, and other everyday matters. He always left those types of decisions up to each autonomous individual.

He defended his disciples when they picked grain on the Sabbath (see Mark 2:23–26). He broke rules about ritual washing (see Matt 15:2–3). He ignored their neglect of fasting (see Matt 9:14–15).

Paul, St. Augustine, and Martin Luther all indicated that if we love God, we can "do as we please" (see Rom 14:5, 14, 22). When Luther said, "Sin boldly," he was reminding us that it's possible to be so fearful of making a mistake that we end up doing nothing! We can be like the proverbial old man who swallowed an egg and afterward was afraid to move lest it should break and afraid to sit still lest it should hatch. That's the lesson we can learn from the one talent man in Jesus's parable. He was severely condemned even though he didn't steal that money or lose that money or waste that money. Actually, he didn't commit any overt sin. He just did nothing (see Matt 25:25–28). Yet Jesus was more critical of him than he was of Zacchaeus, who cheated people, and of the woman who committed adultery.

Life involves some risks. If you wait until motives are absolutely pure and successes are definitely guaranteed, you'll never do anything. No action is free of possible problems. Every move you make will have some negative consequences. To do one thing, you must omit something else. When Jesus stayed in Jerusalem for three days, he caused worry and expense for his parents. Later in his ministry, he often chose to leave needy crowds to meditate. Sometimes he was only able to serve one group by neglecting another. Right versus wrong is not a simple opposite equation. War can be either good or bad. Surgery can be either harmful or helpful. The same knives that can save lives in an operating room can take lives in the back alley. Evil is not a specific entity. Paul said, "I know and am persuaded in the Lord Jesus that nothing is unclean in itself, but it is unclean for anyone who considers it unclean" (Rom 14:14).

Any good thing can become evil if it's perverted or pushed to extremes. In fact, most things are totally amoral, and we must choose whether to use them for good or for evil.

Too often Christians are called "those folks who don't!" A reporter attending an evangelistic conference told some ministers, "I've been here three days, and I know almost everything you guys are against, but I'd sure like to know if there is anything you are for!"

A reasonable religion doesn't have restrictive and limiting regulations. Trivial prohibitions against cultural fads and minor issues are unproductive. Religion should only be concerned with the few actions that cause real harm to people, living things, property, or God's creation. All of us need the freedom to handle decisions about particular situations and personal choices. We don't need rules about unimportant matters.

The subject of miracles is another obstacle that prevents people from understanding the gospel. These ancient accounts were written long before scientific or educational information was available. Therefore, the stories and legends and instructions of the Bible often relate unrealistic, unbelievable events that can only be labeled as superstitions.

These early writers used symbolic expressions much more frequently than our factual-minded researchers and historians do today. They often included poetic quotes, figures of speech, and current idioms that we don't understand. That's why many narratives are so absurd that in our modern world they discredit the valid tenets of our religion. For instance, after God told Adam not to eat from a certain tree in the garden of Eden, a snake advises Eve to disobey this command, saying, "You will not die!" (Gen 3:4).

Later, a donkey talks to Balaam (see Num 22:28–30).

Then a song in Joshua says, "Sun, stand still at Gibeon.... And the sun stood still" (Josh 10:12–13). These passages, and many more like them, are obviously based on idioms or legends.

Also, in dealing with scriptures, we often confuse facts with truth. They are not necessarily synonymous! Some factual statements have far less spiritual significance than the non-factual statement, "You are the salt of the earth" (Matt 5:13).

Thus, literalism becomes another stumbling block. Sometimes the most important question is not, "What did Jesus say?" but rather, "What did Jesus mean?"

The Bible is filled with statements and teachings that require analogous interpretations. We accept many of them quite readily. For instance, when Jesus says, "My sheep hear my voice" (John 10:27), we know he didn't mean these people had four legs and a tail! When he implied we should hate our families (see Luke 14:26), we recognize that this is not a literal commandment. We know it's hyperbole or exaggeration used to make a point. Why, then, are there accusations of heresy when writers or professors suggest that the truth in certain other passages like hell or the second coming may be based on other than factual data?

We must also realize that religion doesn't have a monopoly on truth! Scientific and psychological principles are not inferior to theological principles. Discoveries made in the areas of geology or technology arc to be utilized, not disputed. Christianity has nothing to fear from valid information. Jesus encouraged inquiry and welcomed honest doubt.

Every generation has a right to reexamine and evaluate all the doctrines and practices of their religion without being condemned!

Fantastic answers to prayer are often labeled as miracles. But these dramatic events are erratic and inconsistent. If God answers some requests with supernatural solutions and totally ignores other requests, that creates a problem. If one person is healed of cancer and another one dies, that's a problem. If one family is spared from a tornado and their neighbors are blown away, that's a problem. If your church burns down and the saloon escapes the fire, that's a problem.

Dealing with miracles frustrates believers and forces them to manipulate facts. Well-meaning Christians seem to be constantly trying to fix unfair situations or trying to justify unjustifiable occurrences by saying, "Well, God must have had a reason."

If legends that emphasize miracles are analyzed, however, we'll see that they are often analogies of a profound truth. For instance, when Jesus was baptized, the scriptures don't say a little white bird flew down from heaven and lit on his head. The scriptures only say John saw the Spirit descending "like a dove" and it remained on him.

Now, this occasion was extremely important because Jesus had made a difficult decision to join a religious movement that emphasized righteous behavior and social justice. John's ministry was opening the kingdom to everyone who was willing to repent and follow God's call. In requesting baptism, Jesus was associating himself with people who were considered sinners and outcasts. He was really making a courageous choice to break the rules of society. The intense feelings of God's presence and approval that followed his baptism gave him assurance that this commitment was indeed God's will for his life. John the Baptist used the illustration of a beautiful, peaceful dove to symbolize this indescribable experience (see John 1:32–34).

After his baptism Jesus spent many weeks of intense introspection and soul-searching. He was trying to determine the purpose and mission for his life. He was deciding which methods of ministry he should use to reach people. He was choosing which types of communication would be most effective in transmitting his message of truth. Should he use miraculous means to attract people? Should he attempt dramatic gimmicks to get attention? Should he compromise with religious officials and worldly powers?

The scriptures tell us,

> The tempter came and said to him, "If you are the Son of God, command these stones to become loaves of bread." 4 But he answered, "It is written, 'One does not live by bread alone, but by every word that comes from the mouth of God.'" Then the devil took him to the holy city and placed him on the pinnacle of the temple, saying to him, "If you are the Son of God, throw yourself down, for it is written, 'He will command his angels concerning you,' and 'On their hands they will bear you up, so that you will not dash your foot against a stone.'" Jesus said to him, "Again it is written, 'Do not put the Lord your God to the test.'" Again, the devil took him to a very high mountain and showed him all the kingdoms of the world and their glory, and he said to him, "All these I will give you, if you will fall down and worship me." Then Jesus said to him, "Away with you, Satan! for it is written, 'Worship the Lord your God, and serve only him.'" (Matt 4:3–10)

There is a commonsense explanation for these temptations. Rational people don't believe Jesus confronted some weird creature with horns and a pitchfork during this period in the wilderness. They realize these confusing considerations and possible options were occurring within his own mind. That's where temptations occur. James said, "One is tempted by one's own desire, being lured and enticed by it" (Jas 1:14).

One of these temptations was based on a direct quote from the scripture that says, "For he will command his angels concerning you to guard you in all your ways. On their hands they will bear you up, so that you will not dash your foot against a stone" (Ps 91:11–12).

We know, however, that Jesus didn't regard this passage as a literal promise because he refused to do it. When he recalled Old Testament quotes that seemed to be unreasonable, he always remembered other conflicting passages that nullified them. In this case he refuted the suggestion by quoting the scripture that said, "Do not put the LORD your God to the test" (Deut 6:16). After struggling with various possibilities, he ultimately decided he would avoid miraculous signs and follow a commonsense approach that involved reason and responsibility.

Jesus's overall message had a few major tenets. One was God's universal acceptance of all people. John the Baptist's movement had introduced this idea. He told his followers they could not rely on genetic lineage or special nationality. He insisted Jews had no special favors with God, saying, "Do not begin to say to yourselves, 'We have Abraham as our ancestor,' for I tell you, God is able from these stones to raise up children to Abraham" (Luke 3:8).

Jesus continued this belief and even made a strange statement about heaven that emphasizes inclusion: "In my Father's house there are many dwelling places" (John 14:2). Most people immediately visualize palatial buildings. But Jesus is not describing literal structures in some ethereal paradise. Rather, he is expressing a profound truth. The term *mansion* means a dwelling place, an abode, or a residence. He's assuring us that God has a big tent. His habitat is roomy. It's open to all types of individuals. It's not a cramped or restricted area that allows only a select group of particularly pious people to enter. He explains that the population of God's kingdom is diverse. It includes people "from east and west, from north and south" (Luke 13:29). It also includes "the poor, the crippled, the blind, and the lame" (Luke 14:21). Even publicans, adulterers, prostitutes and thieves, Samaritans, Romans, and Syrophoenicians will be accepted. The ones Jesus called "the least of these" are especially welcomed.

Surprisingly, some of those invited to be residents weren't even aware they had ever interacted with Jesus (see Matt 25:34–39). These people had simply ministered to needy individuals without realizing they were obeying and pleasing God.

This statement about "many dwelling places" gives us a radically different view of God and his kingdom. Peter realized this and said, "I truly understand that God shows no partiality, but in every people anyone who fears him and practices righteousness is acceptable to him" (Acts 10:34–35).

Many incidents reveal how Jesus urged his followers to reach out to marginalized groups. One morning when Jesus found his disciples looking very discouraged, he said, "Friends, have you caught any fish?" They admitted their failure and said, "No."

When it became clear they were not having any success, Jesus gave them some interesting instructions, saying, "Cast the net to the right side of the boat, and you will find some" (John 21:6).

Now, again, Jesus was not being literal. He was not talking about fish. Once more, he was using an analogy. Years before, when he called these followers, even that invitation was not to be taken literally. He had said, "Follow me, and I will make you fishers of people" (Mark 1:17). When he said this, no one envisioned men and women being pulled from the lake on hooks or in nets. They knew this was an analogy.

After "fishing for men" for three years, Jesus had discovered that many people, especially ultra-religious, self-righteous Pharisees, were almost impossible to catch. That's why he urged his followers to fish on a different side of the boat. In other words, he was suggesting that they should reach out to groups of non-religious and unorthodox people, such as publicans and Gentiles.

The overall lesson in this incident teaches us that if one method is unproductive and if one group is unresponsive, we should change our tactics and do something else.

During the great depression, Franklin Delano Roosevelt sent out a group of economic managers with this mission: "Fellows, go out there and do something. If it works, do it some more. But if it doesn't work, do something else."

Jesus would agree.

Another example of Jesus's methods of ministry is revealed in the feeding of the five thousand. It's important to note that the narrative doesn't say Jesus magically created bread from stones. It explains how he used the ordinary resources that were available, namely a child's lunch (see John 6:9). This teaches us we can feed people today by sharing what we have, even if the contribution of each person seems to be small and inadequate.

Some legends probably developed from simple statements. For instance, in the story about "getting money to pay taxes from a fish's mouth," Jesus may have been telling Peter to go and do what he knew how to do to earn the money. Of course, this would be by fishing, since that was his former profession (see Matt 17:27).

Many events may have been mislabeled as miracles because the people did not understand natural laws. In 1900 if you had told someone that in a few years we would be sending pictures through the air, they'd have said, "If so, that would have to be a supernatural miracle." But we do it every day now by using scientific laws.

If a child in the early twentieth century bragged that "when I'm grown, I'll go to the moon," we'd have said, "That would require a supernatural miracle," but several astronauts have done this already.

If a native from a tropical area who wasn't aware of climate change was visiting Alaska in the fall and you told him, "Next month this lake will be so hard, you can walk across it," he would say, "If so, that would have to be a supernatural miracle." But we know that water becoming ice would just be a natural weather phenomenon that the visitor had never seen. One person's miracle may be labeled as a scientific process by a knowledgeable person. Likewise, one person's scientific process may be labeled as a miracle by an uninformed person.

Jesus said, "The blind will see," and they do. Recently, a hospital in Pakistan cured over twelve thousand people of blindness. But it was through medical knowledge and laser surgery, not supernatural miracles. A few years ago, a severe tornado occurred in Oklahoma, but no lives were lost because a radar warning system had recently been installed. That miracle was achieved because of technological knowledge and inventive expertise.

Yes, I believe in miracles, but not in unimportant little magical tricks like staffs that become snakes. I believe in important miracles like an awesome universe filled with starry skies and orbiting planets. I believe in marvelous wonders like the Grand Canyon and Niagara Falls. I believe in even greater miracles when selfish people become generous, when weak people become strong, and when ordinary people do extraordinary things! Those miracles of grace are the real miracles.

In dealing with miracles, we must remember two significant scriptures. First, we know that Jesus doesn't change his character or methods of ministry: "Jesus Christ is the same yesterday and today and forever" (Heb 13:8). Also, the Lord himself says, "The one who believes in me will also do the works that I do and, in fact, will do greater works than these, because I am going to the Father" (John 14:12). If these two statements are true, then whatever Jesus did when he was here on earth must be something we can still do now.

From these promises we know that whatever Jesus did could not have been magical or supernatural because such things do not happen today. If a person claims to raise the dead or walk on water, we laugh. Even so, Jesus was certainly insightful and prophetic when he said that we would do greater things in the future. In the twenty-first century we transplant kidneys and hearts with consistent success. We have drugs that help those with seizures and hallucinations. The only difference is that now we describe these healings in medical terms.

Many of Jesus's wonderful works were probably achieved by his therapeutic approach of acceptance and forgiveness. Other healings may have been based on the placebo effect. We cannot know exactly what happened in every case. But the important thing about Jesus's miracles is that they always showed his deep concern for hurting people. As modern men and women we must realize that these biblical accounts used the vocabulary of that day. Those writers believed conditions such as epilepsy and schizophrenia were caused by internal demons. Therefore, their descriptions included these misguided beliefs. Rather than arguing about the details of these miraculous events, a commonsense gospel should emphasize the fact that Jesus cared for people and ministered to people, and he wants us to do the same.

There are many problems with biblical accounts of miracles when we consider normal human reactions and behavior. For instance, if you were a woman who had a baby without ever being with a man and, furthermore, an awesome angelic visitor had appeared and talked to you about that child (see Luke 1:28–35); then if choirs of angels had filled the sky with songs at his birth (see Luke 2:13); and if strange kings had come to worship him, wouldn't you remember that occasion (see Matt 2:1–12)?

Yet, later, Mary seemed to have no expectation that Jesus was special. She treated him as she would any normal child when he was lost for several days. She didn't immediately look for him at the temple. She admitted she was worried.

Jesus responded, saying, "'Why were you searching for me? Did you not know that I must be in my Father's house?' But they did not understand what he said to them" (Luke 2:49–50). Why on earth wouldn't they understand that he was special if all those miracles had happened at his birth?

Once, Mary and her family even came and interrupted his ministry, probably hoping he would come home when things got dangerous (see Mark 3:31–32). His brothers didn't seem to know anything about his unusual birth. They didn't believe he was divine (see John 7:5). That isn't reasonable.

Then, if you were one of the disciples at Lazarus's tomb and had watched in astonishment as Lazarus came up out of that grave and stumbled up the hill to meet his family, wouldn't you remember such an event (see John 11:43–44)?

Yet none of the disciples seemed to expect God to raise Jesus from the dead. When they were in danger and the Lord was crucified, not one of them said, "Hey, if Jesus is killed, God will probably bring him back to life!"

There was no hint that they believed such a miracle could happen. They didn't wait expectantly at the tomb for three days. Instead, the disciples immediately accepted his death as final and went back to their former lives (see John 21:3).

The scripture says, "[The disciples] did not understand…that he must rise from the dead" (John 20:9–10).

Thomas was adamant in his skepticism: "He said to them, 'Unless I see the mark of the nails in his hands and put my finger in the mark of the nails and my hand in his side, I will not believe'" (John 20:24–25). Why wouldn't he remember that Jesus had raised several people from the dead? That's not reasonable.

Much harm can come from trying to apply a literal interpretation to miracles. We have incidents of families today who kept dead bodies of loved ones in freezers because they believed God would resurrect them. Also, there are reports of groups beating people to rid them of demons. Parents have even allowed their children to die horrible deaths because they expected God to miraculously cure their diseases.

Jesus never meant for us to be naive and stupid. He said, "Be wise as serpents and innocent as doves" (Matt 10:16).

Religion can be dangerous! This is not only true of weird cults. It can be true of any faith that becomes addictive or illogical.

Certain worship practices lead to chemical highs and altered moods. The wonderful emotions teens feel at camp and church members feel at revival crusades always fade. When our brain chemicals that produce excitement and pleasure are depleted, there is always a low period until they can build up again. Rather than accepting this as a natural process, many people try to maintain their highs by manufacturing pseudo-spiritual feelings.

Searching for ecstasy and then experiencing the deep depression that inevitably follows can set up a bipolar pattern. Some individuals become religious junkies constantly looking for a fix. They feel dissatisfied when worship services fail to produce a rush. As the intense feelings invariably fade, these addicts become increasingly vulnerable and in danger of developing other addictions.

Those who become frustrated and dissatisfied will try to find someone to blame. They'll say, "Maybe it's the pastor's fault. Let's get a new preacher." Or "Maybe it's those worldly members' fault. Let's excommunicate them." Or "Maybe it's this organization's fault. Let's change churches." Also, those members who don't experience super-highs all the time are made to feel guilty because they aren't religious enough. It's significant that Jesus never encouraged people to show great excitement or display great emotion.

The conflicts and divisions so common among evangelical churches are a direct result of these unhealthy attitudes. Many disillusioned members eventually leave Christianity forever and pass on a legacy of bitterness to future generations.

As human beings we need stability and balance. We must understand that it's normal for highs to be followed by lows. Of course, we can have inspiring moments, but expecting to live on a mountaintop every day is unreasonable. Jesus didn't promote a dangerous religion. He never urged his followers to have any particular feelings. But he did encourage them to show loving concern and to perform good deeds.

Depending on signs and wonders hinders us from understanding and applying the gospel. Jesus refused to use miraculous means to achieve his mission. He would not perform stunts by leaping from the temple. He also refused to emphasize supernatural events: "The Pharisees came and began to argue with him, asking him for a sign from heaven, to test him. And he sighed deeply in his spirit and said, 'Why does this generation ask for a sign? Truly I tell you, no sign will be given to this generation'" (Mark 8:11–12).

Talking snakes and eight-hundred-year-old prophets are so foreign to us and our way of life that they separate us from the valid and useful scriptures that say "God is love," "Forgive your neighbor," and "Be at peace."

It's tragic that the only things many people think about when you mention Jesus are that a star moved over his manger, he walked on water, and he was crucified and came back to life on Easter. The only things many people know about the Bible is that Eve ate an apple, Noah built an ark, Jonah was swallowed by a fish, David killed Goliath, and Daniel escaped from a lion's den.

We are so concrete-minded that objects we can picture or events we can view in a movie are the only ones we remember. That's one of the dangers of signs and wonders and miracles; they distract us from important teachings. We should go deeper into ethical and spiritual matters, deal with character and relationship issues, and avoid supernatural claims.

Of course, the most consequential miracle in Christianity is the resurrection itself. We can't turn back the clock to discover all the details of that event, and the scriptural account is sketchy. Most people, like Thomas, want to see and touch a physical person. They want to visualize his ascension, even though by now everyone knows there aren't any pearly gates and golden streets above the clouds.

Other individuals, however, are more like the men going to Emmaus. They had trouble recognizing his physical body, but they did identify with his message (see Luke 24:13–33). This type of person may be satisfied just to know that the essence and influence of his spiritual presence is still alive and evident. They are able to see his values reflected in the contributions of people like Dr. Martin Luther King Jr. They can see his compassion revealed in the ministry of people like Mother Teresa. They can see his courage in the lives of martyrs and heroes who die for their cause or country.

They may also remember Jesus's own words when he said, "I am with you always, to the end of the age" (Matt 28:20). They know this statement has not been fulfilled in a literal sense, but when they see his purposes are being achieved and his mission is being carried out, that's enough for them, so either view of the resurrection seems to be valid.

All of us need factual information and honest explanations. Therefore, Jesus's commonsense gospel avoids a lot of negative rules and views miracles as either analogies that teach lessons or as legends.

Chapter 4:

Scripture Is Inspired, Not Inerrant

If anyone dares to question a passage or even a word of the Bible, they can expect well-meaning defenders of the faith to immediately counter by quoting, "All scripture is inspired by God" (2 Tim 3:16).

But most of these people don't realize that when Paul wrote that verse, the Bible as we know it didn't even exist! At that time the term *scripture* simply meant any writing or engraving. Few people were literate, and written material was so rare that any type of script was viewed as something extremely important, and thus believed to be inerrant.

Linguists know it's impossible for any language to be inerrant because words don't have exact definitions. A pinto can be a horse, a bean, or a car. You can either train an animal or ride in a train.

The meanings of words also change drastically over the years. *Gay* and *chip* certainly don't have the same meanings today that they did one hundred years ago.

Then there is the problem of translations. Why would Hebrew and Greek be the only perfectly inerrant languages and all others just have approximate synonyms?

We must understand that many biblical expressions are symbolic. When Jesus called false prophets "ravenous wolves," that wasn't literal (see Matt 7:15–16). When he said, "You must bear much fruit," he didn't mean apples and oranges (see John 15:5). He even said we must "eat his flesh and drink his blood," but we know we are not cannibals or vampires (see John 6:53–54). He validated nonliteral interpretations by saying John the Baptist could be Elijah if you chose to accept the prophecy that way (see Matt 11:14).

An even greater problem with inerrancy involves trying to correlate what God supposedly said in the Old Testament with what Jesus said in the New Testament. For instance, when a man gathered sticks on the Sabbath, the scripture says, "Then the LORD said to Moses, 'The man shall be put to death; all the congregation shall stone him outside the camp.' The whole congregation brought him outside the camp and stoned him to death, just as the LORD had commanded Moses" (Num 15:35–36). But Jesus always refused to honor any of these so-called commandments as inerrant. He said, "The Sabbath was made for humankind" (see Mark 2:27).

The backgrounds and experiences of the hearers also affect how they understand and respond to words. For instance, a child from a loving family will probably have a positive attitude toward the word *father*, but a child from an abusive family may have a negative attitude toward that same word and understand it quite differently.

Common sense causes many people to doubt inerrancy. Cruel commandments, inconsistent statements, and questionable content must all be evaluated. If a wise and loving God was really trying to give us the "wisdom of the universe" in written form, why would he spend so much time and space on trivial matters, such as the length of the fringe on the priest's garment (see Num 15:37–38)?

Also, few readers know that two rather long passages in this infallible and inerrant Bible are word-for-word duplications (see 2 Sam 7:17–29 and 1 Chron 17:15–27). Why would an omniscient God dictate such repetitions?

It's strange that people who are the most vocal about "believing the Bible" often know the least about it. A recent poll showed that only eleven percent of those crusading to keep the Ten Commandments posted in public buildings could even name them! To have credibility, individuals must pay their dues by being informed before they make demands about honoring the scriptures.

Some people's worship of the Bible borders on idolatry. Jesus didn't say, "God is scripture, and you must worship him with paper and ink." He didn't say, "You shall love your Bible with all your heart and soul and mind." In fact, he didn't even mention there would ever be such a holy book! Isn't that strange? Instead, he told us that by using our own instincts, insights, and consciences, we can allow the Holy Spirit within us to be our guide on moral and religious matters.

Knowledgeable readers must admit that trying to claim scriptural inerrancy and infallibility is an impossible task. Many passages are inhumane. Others are almost laughable. Even the inspired writers themselves did not believe in absolute inerrancy. Paul, who wrote much of the New Testament, said, "For we know only in part, and we prophesy only in part.... For now we see only a reflection, as in a mirror, but then we will see face to face. Now I know only in part; then I will know fully, even as I have been fully known" (1 Cor 13:9, 12). This honest Christian is admitting he writes with inadequate and limited knowledge.

Even Jesus disputed many verses that the Old Testament had said were direct quotes from God (see Lev 24:13, 19–20; Matt 5:38–39). Since Jesus bluntly contradicts this Old Testament scripture and certainly doesn't attribute it to a divine source, whose advice should we follow, God's or Jesus's?

There are many other such contradictory statements. The scripture reports that God said, "If a man is discovered lying with the wife of another man, both of them shall die, the man who lay with the woman as well as the woman" (Deut 22:22). Yet when the mob brought the woman taken in adultery to Jesus, he didn't obey this law (see John 8:7, 11).

In the Old Testament, God said, "You shall not eat any detestable thing" Then he relates a detailed list of what is prohibited and what is allowed (see Deut 14:3–20). Yet Jesus said, "Do you not see that whatever goes into a person from outside cannot defile, since it enters not the heart but the stomach and goes out into the sewer?" (Mark 7:18–19). By saying this, Jesus was indicating all foods are suitable for us to eat.

Again, it's recorded that God will choose the place where people should bring burnt offerings (see Deut 12:5–14). Yet Jeremiah later denied this scripture was inerrant by quoting God as saying, "I did not speak to them or command them concerning burnt offerings and sacrifices. But this command I gave them, 'Obey my voice, and I will be your God, and you shall be my people; walk only in the way that I command you, so that it may be well with you'" (Jer 7:21–23).

Later, Jesus went even further, saying, "But the hour is coming and is now here when the true worshipers will worship the Father in spirit and truth, for the Father seeks such as these to worship him. God is spirit, and those who worship him must worship in spirit and truth" (John 4:23–24).

Over and over again, we see Jesus updating, modifying, and contradicting Old Testament commands that were supposedly straight from God's mouth. It's obvious he didn't consider these teachings to be inerrant.

Of course, all Christian groups pick and choose certain scriptures to support their beliefs. Those who require baptism for salvation use "repent and be baptized every one of you in the name of Jesus Christ so that your sins may be forgiven" (Acts 2:38).

Those who practice baptism by sprinkling use "I will sprinkle clean water upon you, and you shall be clean" (Ezek 36:25).

Those who emphasize the Holy Spirit use "all of them were filled with the Holy Spirit and began to speak in other languages" (Acts 2:4).

Those who base salvation on works use "as the body without the spirit is dead, so faith without works is also dead" (Jas 2:26).

Those who base salvation on faith and grace alone use "a person is justified by faith apart from works" (Rom 3:28).

Feminist groups use "there is no longer male and female, for all of you are one in Christ Jesus" (Gal 3:28).

Anti-feminist groups use "women should be silent in the churches" (1 Cor 14:34).

The Bible is diverse. It was written across so many eras and from so many perspectives that almost anything can be proved by some particular passage. Inconsistent and conflicting teachings force people to compartmentalize their lives. If they must believe one way and behave another way, this produces great inner conflict. If what we hear preached on Sunday can't be practiced on Monday, then the church becomes irrelevant.

One businessman said, "Pastor, I enjoy your sermons. On Sunday I go away with my emotions stirred and my heart inspired, but then on Monday morning when the phone starts ringing and real-life activities begin occurring, I can't seem to make the transition." That's why Jesus didn't deal with complicated rituals or involved doctrines. He dealt with everyday things like personal character, harmonious relationships, and productive service.

Most readers only tend to notice and remember those scriptures that are meaningful to them. However, Jesus's commonsense gospel can be relevant in twenty-first century.

We must realize that social customs are constantly changing. By our standards today, both Abraham Lincoln and Harry Truman would be considered racists. Yet Lincoln abolished slavery, and Truman integrated the military. These were giant steps forward for them. This proves that success doesn't necessarily mean achieving a perfect solution. It means taking at least one small step in the right direction. That's why we must consider the inspiration of the scriptures from a progressive viewpoint. Each biblical writer reflected his own level of maturity and the state of his own culture at the time. As people learned more, their moral and ethical values improved.

We would consider Solomon to be a terrible adulterer, with seven hundred wives and assorted mistresses. We would consider the Apostle Paul to be woefully misguided when he ordered slaves to obey their masters and women to be subservient. But according to their social environment, both Solomon and Paul believed these ideas and practices were acceptable. Biblical precepts must be viewed in the context of their era, and our moral guidelines must be adapted as new knowledge becomes available. That's why no written document can ever be the final word in a changing world. It's also why God gave us the Holy Spirit to serve as an inner guide that can go with us as we face new problems in the future.

The practice of quoting isolated Bible verses out of context is also a great hindrance to theological progress. Certain scripture passages are universal favorites among fundamentalist sects. For instance, some groups use "I was born guilty, a sinner when my mother conceived me" (Ps 51:5) to prove mankind's innate depravity.

They use "no one can see the kingdom of God without being born from above" (John 3:3) to prove only born-again religious experiences are valid.

They use "there is no other name under heaven given among mortals by which we must be saved" (Acts 4:12) to prove members of other cultures must become evangelical Christians to be accepted by God.

They use "for the husband is the head of the wife just as Christ is the head of the church" (Eph 5:23) to prove women must be submissive to men.

They use "I do not permit a woman to teach or to have authority over a man; she is to keep silent" (1 Tim 2:12) to prove women can't be church leaders.

They use "those who spare the rod hate their children" (Prov 13:24) to prove corporal punishment is essential.

These verses and many others are used to win arguments and support prejudices, while some texts are completely ignored or avoided.

If the Bible is God's Word, literally true and equally inspired, absolutely inerrant and totally infallible, then why are there so many unpreached texts?

Some texts are not preached because we don't want to hear what they have to say! Moses said, "You will not borrow" (Deut 15:6). Does this mean we shouldn't have mortgages on our homes?

Jesus said, "Sell your possessions, and give the money to the poor.... Then come, follow me" (Matt 19:21). Does this mean we must sell our homes and businesses and give all the money away?

Jesus said, "Do not store up for yourselves treasures on earth" (Matt 6:19). Does this mean we shouldn't have any pension funds or IRA accounts?

Jesus said, "Take no gold, or silver, or copper in your belts" (Matt 10:9). Does that mean we must travel without our wallets or credit cards?

These are astonishing scriptures! They surely can't be taken seriously in the twenty-first century. Most of us skip over these verses by claiming that circumstances have changed. That's fine, but if we do that, then we must be prepared to skip over other verses.

Then some texts are not preached because we are ashamed of them (see Exod 21:20–21; 22:18; Deut 13:6–10; 14:21; 20:12–17; 21:18–21; 23:1; 23:2–3; 25:11–12; Lev 21:16–20; Num 5:11–31).

Finally, some texts are not preached because they are too illogical or trivial to be considered.

"You shall not let your animals breed with a different kind; you shall not sow your field with two kinds of seed" (Lev 19:19). Farmers must be careful about their animals and gardens. They may be sinning.

"You shall not plow with an ox and a donkey yoked together" (Deut 22:10). Are oxen and donkeys mortal enemies?

"You shall not wear clothes made of wool and linen woven together" (Deut 22:11). You'd better check those clothing labels!

"Take nothing for [your] journey except a staff" (Mark 6:8). How's your staff collection? Do you need a new one?

"You shall not round off the hair on your temples or mar the edges of your beard. You shall not make any gashes in your flesh for the dead or tattoo any marks upon you" (Lev 19:27–28). Does your barber understand all these instructions?

"They shall not go near a corpse. Even if their father or mother, brother or sister, should die, they may not defile themselves" (Num 6:6–7). Does this mean we shouldn't attend funerals at certain times?

In these quotes we see inhumane and cruel attitudes. We see crude and vulgar language. We see absurd and superstitious ideas. Unfortunately, they must all be faithfully obeyed if the scriptures are really inerrant and infallible! They must all be included in our proclamation of the gospel if the scriptures are truly inerrant and infallible.

Do you suppose all those inerrancy believers even know these verses are in the Bible?

As honest Christians we must admit we do feel uncomfortable with many passages, so let's not sanctimoniously declare, "If it's in the Bible, I believe it!" or "I preach the Bible from cover to cover." That's not true of anyone, no matter how biblically faithful they claim to be. As honest Christians we must admit we do pick and choose our choice of scriptures. We must admit some of these so-called God-breathed texts are best left unpreached!

Holding on to literal interpretations of scriptures while living in a technological world presents insurmountable problems.

The Bible wasn't meant to be interpreted as a factual and literal document. People don't realize Jesus constantly used words as symbols and presented anecdotes as analogies. To him, sheep and goats weren't just animals. They could represent right or wrong lifestyles (see Matt 25:32).

Bread was not just food. It could be God's Word or even Jesus himself (see John 6:51).

A rock could be a moral foundation (see Matt 16:18).

A cup could be a painful experience (see Matt 26:39).

If so many words and passages have symbolic meanings, then why can't certain other words and passages be symbolic? For instance, why must the "fires of hell" be literal (see Mark 9:44), but the "fires of Pentecost" can simply describe the divine power of the Holy Spirit (see Matt 3:11; Acts 2:3)?

Why must the second coming indicate a specific day when a white-robed man will come floating down from the clouds (see Matt 26:64), but Jesus's promise to be "with us to the end of the age" can simply mean we are aware of his spiritual presence (see Matt 28:20)?

We don't really believe the scriptures are inerrant. We may say we do, but we don't. Our actions reveal our true beliefs!

We teach unbelievable doctrines, but then when some naive Christians try to put them into practice, we're shocked and disturbed.

We scoff at cults who sell all their possessions and gather in groups expecting the rapture. Yet they are obeying the scripture that says, "Keep awake, therefore, for you do not know on what day your Lord is coming" (Matt 24:42).

We view the guy who sits on a mountaintop looking for Christ's appearance in the clouds as a lunatic. Yet the scripture does say, "The sign of the Son of Man will appear in heaven…and they will see the Son of Man coming on the clouds of heaven" (Matt 24:30).

We're even shocked when a bright young student refuses a scholarship to medical school because he believes the end is near. Yet he is basing his decision on the scripture that says, "You also must be ready, for the Son of Man is coming at an hour you do not expect" (Matt 24:44).

We condemn the man who refused to bury his mother because he expected the resurrection. Yet he was remembering that when Jesus said, "Lazarus, come out, the dead man came out" (see John 11:23, 43–44).

We criticize the preacher who relates how he raised a child from the dead during an evangelistic service. Yet we can't deny that Jesus himself said, "The one who believes in me will also do the works that I do" (see John 14:12).

We despise parents who let their children suffer and die instead of seeking doctors or allowing needed surgery. Yet the scripture clearly tells us what do in such a case. It says, "Are any among you sick? They should call for the elders of the church and have them pray over them, anointing them with oil in the name of the Lord. The prayer of faith will save the sick" (Jas 5:14–15).

So what do we really believe? Our normal skeptical reactions to such assertions show what we really believe. They reveal our true feelings about those questionable scriptures.

We must admit that those misguided people who we treat with contempt are being more honest than all the pious hypocrites who claim to believe every word of an inerrant, infallible Bible but never put their money where their mouth is.

If you support and propagate the doctrine of inerrancy, then you have no right to ridicule the poor souls who are vainly trying to live by those unrealistic beliefs.

We give credence to possessions and exorcisms because the scripture says, "The unclean spirits…entered into the swine…and the herd… drowned in the sea" (Mark 5:13). Then, when kids are fascinated by demonology or psychotic criminals commit atrocities "in Satan's name," we're horrified!

What did we expect?

We describe imminent raptures and set dates for millennial events, saying, "This generation will not pass away until all things have taken place" (Luke 21:32). Then, when a politician refuses to support pollution control to prevent global warming because it seems to be a waste of time if the end is so near, we're appalled.

What did we expect?

We say, "You can't trust your senses." We criticize science. We ridicule intellectuals. We condemn doubters and questioners. Then, when teenagers are brainwashed by cult leaders, we're amazed.

What did we expect?

We extol spiritual authority and blind obedience. Then, when well-meaning individuals drink poisoned Kool-Aid with Jim Jones or follow through on the Heaven's Gate suicide pact, we're astonished.

What did we expect?

As Christians, we can't have it both ways! We must not preach things that cannot be lived. We must not hold beliefs that lend themselves to superstitious perversions. Our false teachings will return to haunt us. If you sow nonsense, you'll reap nonsense!

That's what you should expect!

The final criteria is this: If you can't state a belief plainly, proudly, and publicly, then it's probably a faulty doctrine! Those early biblical writers were inspired, but they were not inerrant. Each one wrote what he sincerely believed to be true at that time and place with the knowledge he had. But as more information became available, the writings reflected that growth.

An analogy may illustrate this process. When scientists begin a dig at an archaeological site, the first few days they only find a few clues. If they take a photograph at that point, it will reveal an incomplete and misleading view of the buried city. As they continue to dig, however, more details will be uncovered. Photographs taken later will look entirely different. That doesn't mean the first picture was intentionally deceitful. It was as accurate as it could be at the time it was taken. But it provided an imperfect representation of the buried city. The more the workers uncover, the closer the pictures will be to reality.

Over the years that the scriptures were written, people were maturing, and information was increasing. The prophets changed some concepts. Then Jesus updated many commandments and promised God would continue to reveal his truth to those people who are honest and receptive, saying, "The Advocate…will teach you everything and remind you of all that I have said to you" (John 14:26).

All of us need Jesus's own words of instructions and wise counsel rather than obsolete creeds and contradictory commandments. Therefore, Jesus's commonsense gospel teaches that the scriptures are inspired, not inerrant.

Chapter 5:

The Holy Spirit Makes Us Autonomous

The gospel most of us have heard all our lives fails to give real meaning and relevance to the Holy Spirit. Instead of explaining its vital role as a mental and spiritual guidance system, it's either ignored or considered to be a weird creature associated with doves, fire, and unknown tongues.

Once, a missionary was talking with an elderly gentleman. Finally, the old fellow said, "Sir, God made the world, and I can worship him. Jesus loves me, and I can appreciate him. But that bird—I just don't get it!"

To be honest, almost nobody gets it when they hear current descriptions of the Holy Spirit. It has become one of the most confusing doctrines of the Christian faith.

It's unfortunate that the Holy Spirit has been associated with strange symbols and occurrences. When John said he saw "the Spirit of God descending like a dove," he was attempting to describe an emotional and sacred moment of intense consecration (see Matt 3:16).

When the scriptures say the Holy Spirit "appeared to them as tongues resembling fire which settled on each one of them," this expression was attempting to describe a powerful life-changing event that affected each man and woman personally (see Acts 2:1–3).

In both cases the writer was searching for words to describe the indescribable. The Holy Spirit is the inner motivation that some people today call our conscience, our better angels, our higher self, or our moral compass.

When we think or speak or act in unselfish ways, that's the influence of the Holy Spirit.

When we rise above the animalistic reactions of greed, retaliation, and revenge, that's the influence of the Holy Spirit.

When we do what's right rather than what's easy or pleasurable or financially rewarding, that's the influence of the Holy Spirit.

Commentaries and paraphrased versions of scripture always give several possible synonyms, such as comforter, counselor, helper, intercessor, advocate, and strengthener when they try to define the Holy Spirit. That's because in the first century there were no words to adequately describe this concept. Biological and psychological data about the human mind and body had not been discovered and developed. Even today, information about how this helper can be useful to us is sketchy.

Teachings about the Trinity are an explanation of mankind's three significant steps toward spiritual maturity. The Father, the Son, and the Holy Spirit are not three heads on one body. They aren't necessarily three simultaneous manifestations. Instead, they may be viewed as three phases in a long-term evolving process.

When the prophets finally grasped the fact that the God out there loves and cares for us, they were beginning to glimpse "God the Father." That was the first step.

When the disciples believed in a man who said he was revealing God's character, message, and purpose, they began to comprehend that if God could be embodied in a human being, then perhaps he could be with us! Thus, in Jesus they saw "God the Son." That was the second step (see John 14:9).

Then, when Jesus's followers could sense a divine voice and still feel Jesus's presence even after his death, they began to believe God could really be in all believers. That's when they began envisioning "God the Holy Spirit." This best and highest perception was the third step.

There is no way, however, that men and women could have moved directly from the idea of God as a supreme, powerful deity out there to the idea of God as an intimate, personal spirit in here. Such a momentous understanding had to develop gradually as knowledge and maturity increased. This is one important way in which Jesus, the Christ, became a mediator between God and man.

The day of Pentecost represents an important epiphany. It was an awakening and an enlightenment. In many ways it was the birth of democracy. Some of Jesus's last words were concerning the Holy Spirit. He said, "You will receive power when the Holy Spirit has come upon you" (Acts 1:8). Understanding and utilizing this gift does give us power.

The Pentecost event provided those individuals with encouragement, support, and a sense of authority. It was on this occasion that a large group of people first came to the realization that ordinary men and women can recognize truth, analyze information, make their own decisions, and become autonomous. If we can believe we possess these possibilities and if we can be sure we have a right to use them, then this will indeed give us tremendous confidence and personal power.

On Pentecost the Holy Spirit did remind these disciples of the many promises Jesus had given about their role as believers. He had told them believers would be free and knowledgeable, saying, "I do not call you servants any longer, because the servant does not know what the master is doing, but I have called you friends, because I have made known to you everything that I have heard from my Father" (John 15:15).

He had told them believers would be confident and successful, saying, "All things can be done for the one who believes" (Mark 9:23).

He had told them believers would be in charge of circumstances here on this earth, saying, "if you have faith the size of a mustard seed, you will say to this mountain, 'Move from here to there,' and it will move, and nothing will be impossible for you" (Matt 17:20). That's the kind of power our faith can give us.

At one point during their dramatic experience on that day, the people asked this question: "How is it that we hear, each of us, in our own native language?" (Acts 2:8). This doesn't necessarily indicate these people were instantly grasping the meaning of foreign words and phrases. It may indicate the Holy Spirit enabled each of these normal individuals to perceive and understand spiritual insights that were coming from their own intuition, thoughts, and ideas. It could mean men and women were realizing for the first time that it's possible for us to hear God as he speaks to us through our own memories, urges, and consciences.

Then the illustration of inspired Christians speaking many languages was intended to emphasize that the gospel of Jesus is not for just a few elect individuals of one nation or religion. It's for people of every race and every culture (see Acts 2:7–11). Jesus knew his message would eventually be received by people all over the world, so his teachings would have to be adapted to reach a diverse population. As long as the physical Jesus was here on earth, his followers accepted the fact that God was in him, but they still considered this a phenomenon that belonged exclusively to him. They did not yet regard Jesus as a prototype of what humanity should be. That is why Jesus said, "It is to your advantage that I go away, for if I do not go away, the Advocate will not come to you" (John 16:7). In other words, he was saying, "You will never become autonomous as long as you are relying on me to reflect God. Each of you must reflect God!"

Jesus knew we can't explore new insights, deal with deeper thoughts, or do greater things until we develop our own intellectual capacity. That's why he warned that as long as he was physically available, his followers wouldn't utilize their own resources. They wouldn't rely on their own spiritual intuition. They wouldn't develop their own innate abilities. They wouldn't become free and independent thinkers. They wouldn't strengthen their own relationship with God.

Jesus emphasized the Holy Spirit's role as a messenger from God. He says if we are honestly seeking truth, the Holy Spirit will give us insights and wisdom! James agreed, saying, "If any of you is lacking in wisdom, ask God, who gives to all generously and ungrudgingly, and it will be given you" (Jas 1:5).

This indicates that he expects us to analyze and understand spiritual information. He never requires us to accept unreasonable tenets by faith. He encourages us to rely on our own sense of what's right and to use the brains God has given us.

Some people try to avoid personal accountability by saying we're not supposed to know all spiritual mysteries. They say we can never understand the mind of God. But that's not true! Jesus asked questions at age twelve (see Luke 2:46). He wanted to know then, and he wants us to know now.

Paul agreed we are co-equal with Jesus, telling us God predestined us to be conformed to the image of his Son in order that he might become "the firstborn in a large family" (see Rom 8:29).

He also says the Holy Spirit seeks to empower us from within by helping us use our own bodies and minds. He said, "You may be strengthened in your inner being with power through his Spirit" (Eph 3:16).

Jesus assures us that the Holy Spirit gives us the personal internal strength that enables us to be mature and independent. He urges us to quit depending on external authorities and to begin trusting our own moral faculties.

Therefore, when we need guidance on moral issues, we don't have to always look up a scripture verse or ask a preacher. We can decide for ourselves.

The Holy Spirit is the channel through which we are empowered to use our own natural instincts and intellectual abilities to discover and understand theological information and receive moral guidance.

We're also assured that the Holy Spirit is not a temporary emotional high. This spiritual presence is intended to become a permanent integral part of us.

Toward the end of his time on earth, Jesus taught almost constantly, but he soon realized he wasn't going to be able to cover every subject. He admitted this was a problem when he said, "I still have many things to say to you, but you cannot bear them now" (John 16:12).

What are these things people were not ready to hear? Paul alluded to a similar problem when he said, "I fed you with milk, not solid food, for you were not ready for solid food. Even now you are still not ready, for you are still fleshly. For as long as there is jealousy and quarreling among you, are you not fleshly and behaving according to human inclinations?" (1 Cor 3:2–3).

The explanation in this passage indicates at least some of the solid food we so desperately need may include psychological information about self-discipline and relationship issues. If so, think how much worse such problems have become in the modern era. Our drug culture, the proliferation of guns with mass shootings, and cars with road rage greatly increase the many lethal methods of venting anger.

The writer of Hebrews also deals with this, saying, "For though by this time you ought to be teachers, you need someone to teach you again the basic elements of the oracles of God. You need milk, not solid food.... But solid food is for the mature, for those whose faculties have been trained by practice to distinguish good from evil" (Heb 5:12, 14).

This passage suggests the solid food may also deal with logic, reason, and decision-making skills. Now again, consider the new developments that have made choices so much more complex in our world today. We have television, internet, cell phones, Instagram, Facebook, and dozens of other communication devices that allow propaganda, disinformation, rumors, and bullying threats to reach thousands of individuals instantly. We even have nuclear weapons, drones, and innumerable other methods of destroying humanity.

None of these things were dealt with in the scriptures. They couldn't be because they were not even imagined. But are we dealing with them now? That's the question! Are our churches preaching, teaching, and discussing these crucial issues? This writer says we should be! He encourages us to avoid shallow, pious platitudes and endless repetitions. He tells us we should be analyzing deeper, life-changing moral problems and dealing with modern social and relationship issues.

He says we must get beyond the basic teachings of Christianity. He urges us to move toward spiritual maturity. He tells us we shouldn't have to keep repeating information about repentance, atonement, and faith in God. We know about the resurrection from the dead. We know about judgment and punishment. Since we already know about these things, we should be considering more advanced teachings (see Heb 6:1–3).

This passage may sound like heresy to strictly conservative religious groups because it seems to casually dismiss most of the major religious doctrines that are still being repeated every Sunday in churches today. It's obvious, however, we will not be able to fulfill the great commission until we understand and explain all those advanced teachings that have been neglected for so long.

Jesus knew many cultural and interracial issues would arise in the future. These as-yet-unknown difficulties and obstacles could not be resolved during his earthly life. He couldn't give advice about possible situations that might occur in the centuries to come. He couldn't leave written instructions to be passed on to later generations. So it wasn't possible for a scriptural admonition to be the last word on these hypothetical subjects.

This proves the canon must not be closed and never can be closed because life keeps changing. One major purpose of the Holy Spirit is to enlighten us about unfamiliar matters and help us deal with new developments. Jesus said, "When the Spirit of truth comes, he will guide you into all the truth, for he will not speak on his own but will speak whatever he hears, and he will declare to you the things that are to come" (John 16:13).

Jesus made one surprising prediction about our possibilities when he promised believers would be able to do greater things than he did. Surely we can't surpass Jesus's wonderful works! But maybe we should consider the enormous technical advances that have been made and become aware of the tremendous opportunities available today. Evaluate the worldwide impact of media. Think about the marvelous breakthroughs in medical and surgical techniques. Enumerate the thousands of humanitarian and benevolent organizations that now serve needy populations.

Jesus foresaw that discoveries would occur and progress would be made in the years to come, but he faced one baffling problem: How could wisdom and guidance be provided for those seekers who would live decades and even centuries after he was no longer walking on the earth? How could God's truth be transmitted to these as-yet-unborn men and women after his personal ministry ended? The solution to this problem came through the concept of the Holy Spirit. It's unfortunate that this wonderful internal guide has been grossly neglected and misinterpreted. The Holy Spirit has usually been presented as a supernatural creature because the first century's vocabulary didn't include any terms to describe psychological principles or our brains' conscious and subconscious functions. Few theologians have explained that the Holy Spirit is really a utilization of our own physical, emotional, and spiritual faculties. Paul was trying to explain this concept when he said, "It is that very Spirit bearing witness with our spirit that we are children of God"

(Rom 8:16). He was emphasizing that the Holy Spirit is our connection to God.

Jesus realized there were many things the people of his generation wouldn't be able to understand. He knew not every problem that might arise later could be dealt with during his lifetime here on the earth. He was aware scientific discoveries and technological inventions would continue to create new problems, but things like mass transportation, internet pornography, and space travel were beyond their comprehension.

Paul was also aware that neither he nor any other prophet had perfect religious knowledge. He expected further growth, realizing the little knowledge he had would be replaced by a clearer understanding of truth in the future. He knew that when he had complete and perfect understanding, that which was incomplete and imperfect would become void (see 1 Cor 13:8–12). He also knew any advice he gave at that time would not be valid forever. He admitted future information would eventually make his current instructions obsolete. This honest acknowledgment from Paul gives us both the right and the obligation to continue adapting and updating doctrines in an ever-changing world.

Since Jesus knew we'd have questions and problems after he was no longer physically present, he promised the Holy Spirit's help. This assures us that it's not only permissible but mandatory for modern-day Christians to keep searching for new information, to keep finding answers to theological questions, and to keep developing solutions to humanitarian problems.

The Holy Spirit works through our own minds and hearts. This affects both our intellects and our emotions. It enables us to continue analyzing Jesus's teachings and carrying on his ministry.

Are we using all the powerful assets the Holy Spirit provides? Are we really utilizing the gift of the Holy Spirit in our daily lives?

We must remove the Holy Spirit from the mysterious, theoretical realm and relate it to real life and common sense.

When you have a gut-level warning that cautions you of danger, that may be the Holy Spirit.

When you have an urge to speak a word of encouragement to a needy person, that may be the Holy Spirit.

When you see a problem and feel a sense of responsibility to solve it, that may be the Holy Spirit.

When your conscience enables you to forgive and reconcile with an associate, that may be the Holy Spirit.

When you are anxious and ask God for help, the resulting feelings of assurance may be the Holy Spirit.

When you face difficult decisions and then get new information or notice unusual events that assist you in your choice, that may be the Holy Spirit.

The Holy Spirit is not some strange external force or mysterious phenomenon. Instead, the Holy Spirit works through our own physical, mental, and emotional faculties and gives us access to the wisdom of an omniscient God.

We must believe in possibilities! All great achievements were once unrealized dreams. The giant oak tree lies in the tiny acorn. The majestic eagle crouches inside the fragile egg. A potential saint resides in every sinner.

We must go beyond our comfort zone and broaden our horizons. Once, a woman put her goldfish in a large tub while she cleaned their small bowl. She thought they would enjoy and take advantage of the freedom and space of the bigger environment. Surprisingly, however, they continued to swim in the same little circles their previous container had allowed. They had become conditioned to limitations.

We must not become conditioned to limitations. Paul said, "Do not quench the Spirit" (1 Thess 5:19).

Understanding the role of the Holy Spirit also solves the problem of the unpardonable sin. Jesus said, "People will be forgiven for every sin and blasphemy, but blasphemy against the Spirit will not be forgiven" (Matt 12:31).

This is a confusing and disturbing scripture. We know God forgives all transgressions, but he cannot forgive a person if that individual has deliberately cut off all access to him. The Holy Spirit is our connection to God. If we sever that crucial bond, the relationship is broken, and no further interaction will be possible.

The stubborn refusal to hear and respond to truth is the only unpardonable sin. The scripture calls this hardening the heart.

Disrespecting our internal spiritual messenger, denying the urgings of our God-given conscience, or disregarding the gentle whisper from within is a serious sin.

The writer of Hebrews warns us about this, saying, "Today, if you hear his voice, do not harden your hearts" (Heb 3:7–8).

Faking it, pretending, or closing our eyes to truth is tampering with the controls of our divine guidance system. Suppose a little red light begins to flash on your auto dashboard. Maybe you don't see it; or maybe you see it and ignore it; or maybe you're in a hurry and say, "I'll tend to that tomorrow"; or maybe you take a hammer and break out the bulb, saying, "Now, that's better. It doesn't blink anymore. Everything is great!"

But everything is not great. Things are worse than ever. You didn't fix the problem. You just destroyed the warning device! It's dangerous to ignore your conscience and deceive the Holy Spirit!

The Holy Spirit enables us to fulfill our responsibility as God's agents. It empowers us to carry out the great commission and be a witness to the world.

In one of his last conversations with his disciples, Jesus gives us the authority to be in charge. He said, "You are witnesses.... I am sending upon you what my Father promised, so stay here in the city until you have been clothed with power from on high" (Luke 24:49). This power from on high is the Holy Spirit, and having this divine counselor within assures us that if we are honest, sensitive, and obedient, then our decisions will be legitimate. We don't have to feel guilty about playing God when we encourage scientific discoveries, develop technical advances, or even dare to make revisions in theological areas by putting new wine in new bottles.

All of us need spiritual guidance and encouragement to follow our higher aspirations. The Holy Spirit fills these needs. Therefore, Jesus's commonsense gospel teaches that this personal connection to God makes us autonomous.

Conclusion

There's a lot of unreasonable, unrealistic, and irresponsible nonsense being propagated in the name of religion. Faith healers give false hopes. Evangelists criticize psychology, ridicule science, and censor history. Fanatics exorcize demons and denounce devil worship. Terrorists fight wars, and psychotics commit crimes. All these things are done in the name of God. It's strange that you almost never hear about atheists or unbelievers who kill prostitutes or burn babies or beat children and then claim their ideology caused them to do that! Yet warped religious notions often lead to such atrocities.

Religious organizations are not subject to the same truth in advertisement standards required of other businesses. They aren't held liable in the same malpractice suits that threaten other professions. Absurdities are overlooked, and damage is excused. Legal authorities seem reluctant to challenge theologians. Reporters and editors hesitate to criticize groups with pious labels. There's almost a superstition about negative evaluations of anything that can be classified as religious. Such hesitance is neither wise nor scriptural.

Jesus constantly challenged the temple authorities. He denounced traditional teachings. He warned us about "wolves in sheep's clothing." He also demonstrated that spiritual analysis is not only our privilege; it's our duty: "You will know them by their fruits" (Matt 7:16). *Fruits* means practical results.

Jesus said, "Every tree that does not bear good fruit will be cut down and thrown into the fire" (Matt 7:19). Therefore, effects, not orthodoxy, should be the criteria of all religious doctrines and practices. Before you believe, follow, or support any ideology, always ask yourself these three questions: Is this reasonable? Is this realistic? Is this responsible?

Reasonable things make sense. Reasonable things can be followed to their logical conclusions without any copouts or coverups.

An omniscient God is reasonable! If he's reasonable, then his methods and purposes will be reasonable. Even God is known by his fruits!

Logical people realize it's unreasonable to claim a loving God consigns human souls to eternal perdition. Such a punishment would be vengeance because no rehabilitation is possible at that point.

It's also unreasonable to claim an intelligent God is dogmatic about the minor details of church government, the use of musical instruments, or the specific gender of those who are allowed to preach the gospel. Such trivial doctrinal disputes are incongruent with a reasonable God.

Then, realistic things can be verified by experience. They work! Realistic things produce positive overall long-term benefits.

An omniscient God is realistic. If he is realistic, then all his methods and purposes are realistic. That means when reality conflicts with doctrine, something has to give. We must adjust both elements until they mesh, or we must relinquish one of them. Unfortunately, when reality confronts religion, it's usually reality that suffers. People tend to deny or suppress truth until they see no contradiction.

Christians must hold to the most valid, not necessarily the most comforting, of the two conflicting elements. Paul said, "Test everything; hold fast to what is good" (1 Thess 5:21). To prove means to examine, analyze, and check the evidence. It doesn't mean to swallow or meekly accept. We must be like the blind man who stubbornly stuck to his facts. When he was asked about Jesus, he said, "I do not know whether he is a sinner. One thing I do know, that though I was blind, now I see" (John 9:25).

Jesus said, "We speak of what we know and testify to what we have seen" (John 3:11). God doesn't want us to deny our senses to remain orthodox.

Finally, responsible things strengthen people. They call forth the highest and the best in each individual. Responsible things achieve ultimate good for all involved.

An omniscient God is responsible. If he is responsible, then all his methods and purposes will promote responsibility. That means we will succeed because of our own determination and effort, not because we bribed God to bestow a blessing. We will fail because of our own ignorance and negligence, not because the devil or something else made us do it.

Paul said we should renew our minds to determine what is good and acceptable and perfect (see Rom 12:2).

He also said we are individually accountable: "All must test their own work.... You reap whatever you sow" (Gal 6:4, 7).

God's laws are reasonable, not arbitrary. God's processes are realistic, not mysterious. God's desire for men and women includes autonomy and responsibility, not submission and subordination. We can be autonomous and responsible because God shares his wisdom with us. Jesus said, "To you it has been given to know the secrets of the kingdom of heaven" (Matt 13:11).

In medicine, if a treatment isn't helpful, we change it. In education, if a method doesn't increase a child's knowledge and ability to learn, we change it. In agriculture, if the fertilizer we're using doesn't produce healthy growth, we change it. It's only in religion that we insist upon maintaining traditional beliefs and practices even if they are hurting us, harming others, and creating social problems. It's only in religion that we can't stop and evaluate and change.

It's obvious our world is not as religious as it was in the past. Scientists today are discovering many of the natural principles that explain our universe. We no longer have to rely on supernatural miracles to account for storms and earthquakes and volcano eruptions. As modern men and women, we are relatively autonomous. When we feel capable of controlling our own destinies, traditional belief systems lose some of their appeal.

Nevertheless, we can't dismiss the idea of spirituality that easily. There are valid aspects that even skeptical agnostics must consider. In the first place, nothing comes from nothing. That's not reasonable. Things don't just get better by themselves. The opposite usually happens. A garden left to itself degenerates into a weed patch. A broken engine never makes its own repairs. A jigsaw puzzle doesn't put itself together. Yet life forms have steadily evolved, developed, and improved. Even though order is not evident in every detail of life, it is evident in overall patterns.

Also, our intense desire to know is not always physically rewarding. So why do we have this desire? Our appreciation for beauty in art and harmony in music is not always materially rewarding. So why are we drawn to beauty? The hunger for more and our longing for union with infinity expresses itself in superstitions like channeling, extraterrestrials, and seances. Since interest in such things is a universal phenomenon, it must have a cause.

We know believing in blind chance with eventual annihilation is psychologically debilitating and nonproductive. That's why a commonsense spiritual faith that is reasonable, realistic, and responsible can be a positive element in humanity's progressive development.

Religion's greatest intellectual problem concerns evil. Ancient theology held three basic beliefs: God is all-powerful; God is good; therefore, if I am good, I'll be rewarded. As long as life is fair, with bad people being punished and good people being rewarded, this theology could be accepted. But once bad things happened to a good person, this theology crumbled. That's what the story of Job is all about. If Job is good and bad things happen to him, then that proves one of two things: If God is truly all-powerful, then he is not good; or if God is truly good, then he is not all-powerful. To believe that God is both all-powerful and good, then Job had to be bad. He had to deserve the punishment he received.

At that point the credibility of traditional theology hung in the balance. That's why Job's advisors insisted he must have sinned. They preferred to condemn him rather than to rethink and change their belief system.

Philosophers still ask, "If God is both good and powerful, why do evil things happen?" There are three answers to this question: God is not a dictator, and he is only in charge of spiritual things. Nature is a morally neutral system that's not always fair and righteous. Human beings are in charge of things on this earth, and they make mistakes.

So it's true that everyone experiences isolated incidents that seem tragic and senseless! But from the timeless holistic perspective, even these adversities can "work together for good" (see Rom 8:28).

Many bad things do happen to good people. Jesus was crucified, and Stephen was stoned. Teenagers are killed in accidents, and babies die of cancer. Even so, these lives are not wasted. They are not lost in a universal scenario of chaos. They make us think!

For instance, when a burglar is shot or an alcoholic has liver failure, we say, "That's what they deserved." Such occurrences pose no moral dilemma because we feel these victims are receiving the logical consequences of their actions. These situations don't make us think or search for answers.

It's only when a totally unjustified death or loss is suffered that we are jolted out of our apathy. At times like that, we go deeper in empathy; we analyze circumstances; we look for meaning; we develop solutions; we change and grow.

Thus, every life has a purpose. Every tragic, unreasonable event has a lesson to teach and a redemption to accomplish. These heartbreaking God questions serve as moments of truth. Without them, humanity would never mature.

When Jesus said, "I came to bear witness to the truth," he meant, "I came to replace superstitious notions with reasonable thoughts. I came to deal with reality, not mystical theories. I came to enable believers to be responsible agents, not submissive slaves."

This is the only kind of faith that will survive in our world today. It's the only kind of religion that will succeed in this scientific age. It's the only kind of gospel that will be relevant enough to attract this secular generation.

The teachings of a twenty-first-century church must pass several truth tests. It must present facts, not fantasies. It must provide honest answers to difficult questions. It must offer practical solutions to current problems. And most importantly, all its principles and precepts must be useful to ordinary men and women when they apply them in their everyday lives.

Many of the traditional doctrines of Christianity are becoming obsolete. The conventional rituals are losing their influence. The pious expressions of orthodox ministers are being ignored or ridiculed. The language of Zion is not understood by the people on the street.

Many of these old teachings were important in the development of religious doctrines. They served a real purpose in their era. Some of them were necessary insights that became steppingstones to get people beyond the sacrificial systems and idol worship. But they were not the complete and final word. So it's time for us to go further. Several scriptural writers spoke of this. Joel, and later Peter, who both lived in a male-dominated world, foretold that gender equality and spiritual enlightenment would be available to all in the future (see Acts 2:17–18).

Then Jesus changed many of the rules and precepts. For instance, he would often declare, "It's been said of old," and then go on to repudiate and update commands.

He also gave us permission to learn, grow, and advance, explaining that through the Holy Spirit, God would enable us to rely on our own mental abilities and personal experiences in making moral choices. This Holy Spirit operates within us as a conscience or moral compass. Jeremiah expressed it this way: God said, "I will write [my law] on their hearts" (Jer 31:33).

So what are those things Jesus said the disciples were not ready to hear? What are those advanced teachings the scripture advises us to consider? Are we discovering, developing, and expressing this new information? That is the question!

Since we realize theology has not kept up with the increase in secular knowledge and has not been allowed to grow and change with the times, how can we solve these problems and get beyond these hindrances?

Perhaps the time has come for us to discover, develop, and proclaim Jesus's commonsense gospel that ordinary people can understand and accept. Perhaps we should present the gospel Jesus would present if he were here today.

First, this gospel would describe God as a wise, fair, and loving creator—the God that Jesus revealed and called "Abba, Father."

Second, this gospel would offer a free and reasonable plan of salvation that helps us realize and accept our true position as children of God.

Third, this gospel would abolish negative and destructive doctrines and rules that deal with trivial matters. It would also treat miracles as either analogies or legends.

Fourth, this gospel would view the scriptures in a progressive manner, as inspired but not inerrant and infallible. Furthermore, Jesus's own words should take precedence over ancient passages.

Finally, this gospel would help us realize the Holy Spirit enables us to become spiritually autonomous. It reminds us that when Jesus said, "I have other things to tell you," he was assuring us that, even now in the twenty-first century, believers must continue to discover spiritual insights and put new wine into new bottles.

An egg provides a wonderful parable of gospel flexibility. The shell is a suitable and necessary covering for the chick embryo at a certain stage of its existence, but it's totally unsuitable later on! In fact, at some point that shell must be broken for the bird to survive. The shell is not destroyed because it is wrong or evil. It is destroyed because it has served its purpose and now change is right and good and necessary!

It's the same with the gospel. We don't have to apologize for outgrowing certain beliefs. We don't have to feel guilty about changing our theological perspectives. We don't have to justify our need to develop and present a revised commonsense gospel.

If we fail to change, if we refuse to break the shell of our orthodox and obsolete opinions when they become hindrances to growth, then we are resisting the Holy Spirit, and that's fatal!

As Christian men and women, we are responsible for discovering, analyzing, and dealing with those future issues and advanced teachings Jesus spoke about. We are also responsible for sharing this commonsense gospel. Presenting the gospel as Jesus would if he were here now is exactly what this book is attempting to do.